From Poverty to Prosperity

A CEO's Guide to Fighting Poverty Through Business, Leadership, and Innovation

Turning Vision into Action, and Action into Impact

By

Dr. Tekemia Dorsey

From Poverty to Prosperity (Book 1)

DTD Enterprises, LLC
1 Olympic Plaza Towson, MD 21204

Published 2025
1st Edition
Printed in the United States of America

ISBN: 978-1-958785-20-1 (Hard Cover Printed)
ISBN: 978-1-958785-21-8 (EBook)
ISBN: 978-1-958785-22-5 (Paper Back Printed)

FOREWORD

Poverty is one of the most pressing challenges of our time. It impacts individuals and families in every community, limiting opportunity, stifling potential, and creating barriers to prosperity that can last generations. Yet, it is not permanent. Poverty can be broken—when leaders decide to confront it with courage, vision, and action.

Here in Maryland, we have seen what can happen when leaders make bold choices—whether through education, workforce development, or expanding economic opportunity. But we also know that the government alone cannot solve poverty. We need businesses that innovate with purpose. We need schools and nonprofits that build skills and opportunity. We need communities and faith leaders who inspire resilience and hope. Above all, we need leaders—emerging and established—who refuse to accept poverty as unsolvable.

That is why this book matters. In *"From Poverty to Prosperity,"* Dr. Tekemia Dorsey issues a call to leaders everywhere. Her Vision → Action → Impact framework reminds us that change begins with bold vision, is sustained by decisive action, and is measured by lasting impact. This is not a theory. It is a practical model tested in communities, businesses, and initiatives that have transformed lives.

This book speaks to CEOs and policymakers, but also to teachers, pastors, nonprofit directors, grassroots organizers, and anyone in a position of influence. It challenges all of us to lead—not tomorrow, but today.

I encourage you, the reader, to take this call personally. Reflect on your own sphere of influence—whether in the boardroom, the classroom, the pulpit, or in your community. Consider how you can apply these lessons to create opportunity, to build prosperity, and to ensure that no generation inherits the limits of poverty.

Because poverty can be broken. And together, through leadership, vision, and partnership, we can be the ones to break it.

The Honorable Kim Ross
Delegate, Maryland House of Delegates

Dedication

To my children — **Heaven, Halee, Beloved Joshua, and Brandon —**

You are my heart's greatest work and my life's most important leadership assignment.

You have each taught me the meaning of resilience, hope, and love in its purest form.

May this book be a reminder that no dream is too bold, no challenge too great, and no barrier unbreakable when you lead with courage and vision.

Everything I fight for — every life touched, every community transformed — is, in part, a gift to you and the generations that will follow.

May you always know that the path from *poverty to prosperity* is not just possible… it's your birthright to walk in, and your legacy to extend to others.

With all my love,

Mom

Acknowledgments

Writing this book has been a journey of reflection, gratitude, and renewed commitment — and it would not have been possible without the people who have poured into my life along the way.

First, to my children — **Heaven, Halee, Beloved Joshua, and Brandon** — you are my constant motivation and my most important reason for pressing forward. Your resilience, laughter, and unwavering belief in me are the wind at my back. You remind me daily that the legacy we build is not only for ourselves but for those who come after us.

To my family and loved ones, thank you for your patience, encouragement, and grace during the many late nights and early mornings spent writing, researching, and traveling. Your understanding has been a silent but steady anchor.

To my mentors and coaches, who sharpened my vision and challenged me to think bigger — your belief in my ability to lead change has been a gift I will never take for granted.

To my colleagues, partners, and collaborators in business, education, workforce development, and community transformation — your commitment to real solutions, not just conversations, has inspired every chapter of this book.

To the communities I have had the honor to serve — in boardrooms, classrooms, training halls, and grassroots gatherings — you have shown me repeatedly that poverty does not define potential. Your stories are the heartbeat of this work.

And finally, to every leader and aspiring leader holding this book: thank you for caring enough to act. This work will not be finished by one voice, but by a chorus of leaders willing to turn vision into action, and action into lasting impact.

With deep gratitude,
Dr. Tekemia Dorsey

Letter from the Author

Dear Reader,

Before you turn another page, I want you to know something: **poverty is not permanent**. I don't say that as a distant observer or as someone who has only studied the issue from afar. I say it as someone who has seen it, felt it, and worked alongside countless people determined to break it.

I have walked through neighborhoods where opportunities seemed locked behind unshakable doors — and I have also stood in rooms where those same doors were finally flung wide open. I have watched people discover their talents, build thriving businesses, and create futures for their families that once felt impossible.

This book was born from that tension — the hard truth of poverty's reach, and the unstoppable power of human potential when given the chance to rise. It is my blueprint for leaders at every level — whether you run a global corporation, a local nonprofit, a school, a church, or simply have influence in your own community — to move from **Vision → Action → Impact** in a way that creates lasting change.

You will find stories here. You will find strategies. But most importantly, I hope you will find a challenge — a challenge to use your voice, your skills, your resources, and your leadership to make poverty not just less visible, but less possible.

The path from poverty to prosperity is not paved by one person alone. It takes leaders — bold, collaborative, committed leaders — to see it through. My hope is that, by the time you reach the final page, you will know exactly where you can start, and that you will feel the courage to take that first step.

Thank you for picking up this book. Thank you for caring. And thank you, in advance, for leading.

With purpose and hope,
Dr. Tekemia Dorsey

Table of Contents

FOREWORD.. III

Dedication V

Acknowledgments...VI

Letter from the Author...VIII

Introduction – The Foundation of From Poverty to Prosperity1

The Fourteen Pathways to Breaking Poverty 1

From Pathways to Framework.. 4

Why This Book Is the Next Step.. 5

Chapter 1 – The Leadership Mandate.. 7

Why Leadership Matters More Than Ever................................... 7

The Difference Between Leadership and Position 7

The Moral and Economic Imperative... 8

Your Role in the Mandate 8

Chapter 2 – Breaking Limiting Beliefs...................................... 10

The Invisible Walls Around Us... 10

How Limiting Beliefs Take Root 11

Replacing Limiting Beliefs with Empowering Truths.............. 11

Your Role as a Belief-Breaker... 12

From Mindset Shift to Movement 12

Chapter 3 – Innate Skillset Development 14

Why Skills Matter More Than Resources Alone....................... 14

The Power of Innate Skills... 14

From Hidden Talent to Marketable Strength............................ 15

Why Leaders Must Lead This Process 15

The Ripple Effect of Skill Development 16

Looking Ahead.. 17

Chapter 4 – Youth Development as the Cornerstone............. 18

Why Start with Youth?.. 18

The Cost of Neglect.. 18

Building Effective Youth Development Programs.................... 19

The Leadership Role in Youth Development 20

Case Example: From Youth Leader to Community Leader . 20

A Foundation for Everything Else............................ 21

Chapter 5 – Advocacy and Civic Leadership........................ 22

Why Advocacy Matters in the Fight Against Poverty.............. 22

The Misunderstanding About Advocacy................................. 22

Building Civic Leaders from the Ground Up 23

The Leader's Role in Advocacy............................... 24

From Voice to Victory 24

Looking Ahead.. 25

Chapter 6 – Leadership Training & Development.................. 26

Why Leadership Development Is Essential to Ending Poverty 26

The Gap in Leadership Preparedness 26

Core Elements of Effective Leadership Training 27

Creating a Leadership Pipeline.................................. 28

Case in Point 28

From Training to Transformation.............................. 29

Chapter 7 – Education Pathways: From College to Career 30

Why Education Must Lead to Opportunity.......................... 30

The Disconnect Between Education and Employment............. 30

Building Effective Education-to-Career Pipelines 31

The Role of Leaders in Strengthening Pathways........................ 32

A Vision for Generational Change 32

Looking Ahead.. 33

Chapter 8 – Business Education & Entrepreneurship 34

From Employee to Employer: Expanding the Vision................ 34

The Power of Business Literacy.. 34

Entrepreneurship as a Poverty Breaker 35

Integrating Business Education into Community Development35

A Culture of Possibility.. 36

From Small Businesses to Economic Engines........................... 36

Looking Ahead.. 37

Chapter 9 – Workforce Development & Employment Pathways
.... 38

Why Workforce Development Matters 38

The Workforce Readiness Gap.. 38

Core Components of Effective Workforce Development.......... 39

The Leader's Role in Workforce Pathways............................... 40

Case Example: Aligning Skills with Opportunity 40

From Job Placement to Career Growth 40

Looking Ahead.. 41

Chapter 10 – Financial Wealth Development 42

From Earning to Building... 42

Why Financial Wealth Matters.. 42

Core Elements of Wealth Development 43

Breaking Cultural and Systemic Barriers 43

Teaching Wealth as a Community Value................................... 44

From Survival to Legacy... 44

Looking Ahead.. 45

Chapter 11 – Health & Wellness as a Prosperity Driver 46

Why Health Is Wealth 46

The Poverty–Health Connection 46

Core Areas of Wellness for Lasting Prosperity 47

The Role of Leaders in Promoting Wellness 48

The Economic Impact of Wellness..................................... 48

From Surviving to Thriving... 48

Looking Ahead.. 49

Chapter 12 – Parental Program Development........................ 50

Why Parents Are the Cornerstone of Prosperity................ 50

The Link Between Parenting and Poverty Outcomes.......... 50

Core Components of Effective Parental Programs.............. 51

The Role of Leaders in Supporting Parents....................... 52

Case Example: Whole-Family Impact................................ 52

From Parent Support to Generational Change................... 52

Looking Ahead.. 53

Chapter 13 – Sports, Education & Leadership........................ 54

More Than a Game.. 54

Why Sports Are a Unique Opportunity 54

The Risk Without Integration 55

The Role of Leaders in Leveraging Sports for Change 56

Case Example: Teamwork Beyond the Field 57

From the Field to the Future.. 57

Looking Ahead.. 57

Chapter 14 – Building & Sustaining Community Relationships
.... 58

Why Relationships Are the Glue of Transformation 58

The Foundation of Trust... 58

The Benefits of Strong Community Networks 59

Strategies for Building and Sustaining Relationships.............. 59

The Role of Leaders as Bridge Builders.................................... 60

    Case Example: A Network That Outlasted the Grant............ 60

Relationships as a Long-Term Asset 61

Looking Ahead... 61

Chapter 15 – The Power of Civic Engagement 62

Why Civic Engagement Is Non-Negotiable 62

Beyond Voting.. 62

The Benefits of Active Participation 63

The Leader's Role in Civic Engagement.................................... 63

Overcoming Barriers to Engagement 64

    Case Example: From Silence to Influence.............................. 64

Civic Engagement as a Path to Systemic Change 65

Looking Ahead... 65

Chapter 16 – Scaling Impact Through Innovation................... 66

Why Innovation Is Essential for Growth................................... 66

The Challenge of Scaling 66

Types of Innovation That Drive Scale....................................... 67

The Leader's Role in Driving Innovation.................................. 67

    Case Example: Technology-Enabled Expansion................... 68

From Innovation to Transformation 68

Looking Ahead... 68

Chapter 17 – Measuring Success and Adapting 70

Why Measurement Matters 70

Defining What Success Looks Like 70

Tools and Methods for Measuring Impact 71

The Role of Adaptation in Sustaining Impact 71

Case Example: Course-Correcting for Greater Results . 72

Closing the Loop.. 73

Global Transition into Prologue.. 75

Prologue – The Leadership Imperative to End Poverty 77

From Witness to Warrior: Why I Lead This Work.................... 77

The True Cost of Accepting Poverty... 78

From Management to Mastery: Breaking the Cycle................. 79

The Global Leadership Gap... 80

The Vision → Action → Impact Model 81

A Global Call to Lead... 82

Part I – The Leadership Foundation...................................... 84

Chapter 1 – Harnessing Innate Potential: The Leader's Role in Unlocking Human Capital.. 85

The Untapped Wealth in People.. 85

Innate Skills: The Hidden Power in Every Person 86

Example: Barefoot College, India 86

What Are Innate Skills?.. 86

Why Leaders Must Focus on Skill Discovery........................ 87

The Skill Development Cycle.. 88

Bridging the Gap Between Talent and Opportunity 89

The Role of Soft Skills... 89

Removing Barriers to Skill Development 90

A Story of Transformation 90

Why Innate Skillset Development Is a Poverty Breaker 91

Looking Ahead 91

Why Leaders Must Champion Skill Discovery 92

From Discovery to Development 92

Case Study: Rwanda's Digital Ambassadors Program 93

The Leadership Mindset Shift 93

Global Leadership Insights 94

Call to Action for Leaders 94

Chapter 2 – Youth Empowerment as a Global Economic Strategy 96

The Untapped Engine of Growth 96

Why Youth Development is an Economic Imperative 97

From Passive Recipients to Active Leaders 97

Case Study: Rwanda's YouthConnekt 98

The Role of Leadership in Youth Empowerment 98

Global Examples of Youth-Driven Transformation 99

Leadership Mindset Shift 99

Call to Action for Leaders 99

Chapter 3 – Leadership as Advocacy: Influencing Systems for Lasting Change 101

Why Advocacy is Non-Negotiable for Leaders Fighting Poverty 101

From Charity to Systemic Change 101

Case Study: Brazil's Bolsa Família Program 102

The Leadership Skills Behind Effective Advocacy 103

Global Examples of Advocacy in Action 103

The Role of Business Leaders in Advocacy 104

Call to Action for Leaders 104

Chapter 4 – Transformative Leadership Training: Equipping
Leaders to Dismantle Poverty 106

Why Leadership Development is a Poverty Reduction Strategy
.... 106

From Positional Power to Transformational Influence 106

Case Study: Singapore's Leadership Pipeline 107

The Leadership Gap in Poverty Solutions........................... 107

Core Competencies for Poverty-Focused Leadership 108

Global Examples of Leadership Training Impact 108

Building a Scalable Leadership Development Model......... 109

Call to Action for Leaders 109

Part II – Education and Opportunity.. 111

Chapter 5 – Expanding Horizons: College Exploration as a
Pathway to Prosperity 112

Why Higher Education Access Matters in the Fight Against
Poverty 112

The Access Gap.. 112

From Awareness to Aspiration.. 113

Case Study: The Posse Foundation, USA............................ 113

The Leadership Role in Expanding Access 114

Global Examples of Higher Education Access Efforts 114

Aligning Higher Education with Economic Opportunity . 115

Call to Action for Leaders 115

Chapter 6 – Career Readiness Development: Building
Pathways to Sustainable Employment..................................... 117

Why Career Readiness Is More Than Job Training................. 117

From Short-Term Employment to Long-Term Growth... 117

Case Study: Germany's Dual Education System................. 118

Barriers to Career Readiness in Low-Income Communities
.... 118

The Leadership Role in Career Readiness 119

Global Examples of Career Readiness Initiatives............... 119

Measuring Success in Career Readiness............................. 120

Call to Action for Leaders 120

**Chapter 7 – Business Education as a Tool for Inclusive
Economic Growth**... 122

Why Business Education Matters in Poverty Reduction 122

From Hustle to Sustainable Enterprise 122

Case Study: Goldman Sachs 10,000 Women Initiative 123

Barriers to Business Education Access................................ 123

The Leadership Role in Expanding Business Education.... 124

Global Examples of Business Education Impact 124

Aligning Business Education with Inclusive Growth.......... 125

Call to Action for Leaders 126

**Chapter 8 – Workforce Development Education: Aligning
Skills with the Global Economy** 127

Why Workforce Development Is Central to Breaking Poverty
.... 127

From Skills Training to Workforce Systems....................... 128

Case Study: Switzerland's Vocational Education and Training
(VET) Model 128

**Challenges in Workforce Development for Low-Income
Communities** 129

The Leadership Role in Workforce Development 129

Global Examples of Workforce Development Excellence. 130

Workforce Development as Economic Policy 130

Call to Action for Leaders 131

Part III – Health, Family, and Community 132

Chapter 9 – Health & Wellness: Building the Physical and
Mental Foundations for Prosperity 133

Why Health Is an Economic Issue 133

The Vicious Cycle of Poor Health and Poverty 133

Case Study: Thailand's Universal Coverage Scheme 134

Mental Health: The Overlooked Factor 134

The Leadership Role in Health Equity 135

Global Examples of Health-Driven Poverty Reduction 135

Health as a Productivity Multiplier 136

Call to Action for Leaders 136

Chapter 10 – Empowering Parents: Building Family Stability
as a Catalyst for Prosperity 137

Why Parenting Support Is a Poverty Reduction Strategy 137

The Generational Impact of Parental Empowerment 138

Case Study: Brazil's Criança Feliz Program 138

Challenges Faced by Parents in Low-Income Communities
.... 139

The Leadership Role in Parental Empowerment 139

Global Examples of Family-Centered Approaches 140

Family Stability as a National Asset 140

Call to Action for Leaders 141

Chapter 11 – Building & Sustaining Community Relationships:
The Social Infrastructure of Prosperity 142

Why Social Capital Is as Valuable as Financial Capital.......... 142

The Link Between Community Cohesion and Poverty Reduction 142

Case Study: Medellín, Colombia.. 143

Challenges to Building Community Relationships in Poverty-Affected Areas 143

The Leadership Role in Strengthening Community Networks 144

Global Examples of Social Capital in Action 144

Community as an Economic Multiplier............................... 145

Call to Action for Leaders 145

Chapter 12 – Sports, Education & Leadership: Harnessing the Power of Play for Social Mobility 146

Why Sports Are More Than Games................................... 146

From the Playing Field to the Boardroom 147

Case Study: Right to Play 147

The Role of Sports in Education Access 147

Challenges in Leveraging Sports for Social Mobility 148

The Leadership Role in Sports Development...................... 148

Global Examples of Sports as a Catalyst for Change......... 149

Sports as a Leadership Incubator 149

Call to Action for Leaders 150

Part IV – Systems, Advocacy, and Wealth 151

Chapter 13 – Civic Engagement & Leadership: Mobilizing Communities for Policy and Change............................. 152

Why Civic Engagement Is a Cornerstone of Poverty Reduction 152

From Participation to Leadership.................................... 152

Case Study: Participatory Budgeting in Porto Alegre, Brazil 153

Barriers to Civic Engagement in Low-Income Communities 153

The Leadership Role in Strengthening Civic Engagement 154

Global Examples of Civic Leadership in Action 154

Civic Engagement as a Poverty Disruptor 155

Call to Action for Leaders 155

Chapter 14 – Financial Wealth Development: Turning Economic Gains into Generational Prosperity 157

Why Wealth, Not Just Income, Breaks the Poverty Cycle 157

The Difference Between Income and Wealth 158

From Financial Literacy to Financial Empowerment 158

Case Study: Singapore's Central Provident Fund (CPF) 159

Barriers to Wealth Development 159

The Leadership Role in Wealth Development 160

Global Examples of Wealth Development Initiatives 160

Wealth as a Tool for Equity 161

Call to Action for Leaders 161

Chapter 15 – Cross-Sector Partnerships: Scaling Solutions Beyond Borders 162

Why Collaboration Is the New Currency of Leadership 162

The Global Scale of Partnership Impact 162

Case Study: Gavi, the Vaccine Alliance 163

Leadership Strategies for Building Partnerships 164

Call to Action for Leaders 164

Chapter 16 – Measuring What Matters: Impact, Accountability, and Legacy 166

XXI

Why Measurement Is the Core of Leadership 166

From Outputs to Outcomes 166

Case Study: Vietnam's Multi-Dimensional Poverty Index
(MPI).. 166

Leadership Strategies for Impact Measurement 166

Call to Action for Leaders 166

Next Steps – From Vision to Action to Impact....................... 166

The Work Is Urgent. The Work Is Possible. 166

The Vision to Action to Impact Framework in Practice 167

The Leader's Mandate.. 167

Global Urgency, Local Action 168

Your Next Steps... 168

An Invitation to Join the Movement 169

From Global Perspective to Leadership Ownership 170

The Leadership Imperative... 172

Accountability as the Engine of Change............................. 172

Action that Transforms.. 173

A Call to Leaders and Aspiring Leaders Alike 173

The Charge 174

*PART I: The Leadership Mandate: Answering the Call to Break
Poverty* 176

**Chapter 1 – The Leadership Mandate: Owning the Fight
Against Poverty** 177

From Global Crisis to Personal Responsibility........................ 177

Leadership as a Poverty-Breaking Force 178

The Five Commitments of a Poverty-Breaking Leader .. 178

Bridging Global Lessons and Local Realities................. 180

Why This Mandate Cannot Wait..................................... 181

Your Role, Your Reach, Your Responsibility 181

Chapter 2 – Vision: Seeing Beyond the Present...................... 183

Why Vision is the First and Greatest Act of Leadership 183

The Anatomy of a Poverty-Breaking Vision 183

  Case Study 2: Vision 2020 – Rwanda's National Transformation... 185

  Case Study 3: Grameen Bank – Financial Inclusion for the Poorest... 186

Building Your Own Vision: A Leader's Blueprint.................. 186

From Vision to Alignment 187

  A Challenge to the Reader... 188

Chapter 3 – Action: Turning Vision into Measurable Progress 189

Why Action Is the True Test of Leadership 189

The Three Pillars of Action in Poverty-Breaking Leadership 189

  Case Study 1: Medellín's Integrated Transport System191

  Case Study 2: India's Rural Solar Electrification   191

From Action Lists to Action Culture...................................... 192

Overcoming the Three Enemies of Action.............................. 193

Measuring as You Move 193

The Leadership Shift: From Dreamer to Builder.................... 194

A Challenge to the Reader... 194

Chapter 4 – Impact: Measuring What Truly Matters 196

Impact as the Leader's Legacy... 196

Defining True Impact... 196

  Case Study 1: Vietnam's Holistic Poverty Reduction

Program 197

Case Study 2: Brazil's Bolsa Família Program 198

From Data to Decisions 198

The Risk of Mistaking Activity for Impact 199

Building an Impact Culture 200

Case Study 3: The Graduation Approach 200

The Leader's Responsibility in the Impact Stage 201

A Challenge to the Reader 201

Chapter 5 – Leading Beyond Yourself: Securing a Legacy of Change 203

Why Leadership That Lasts Must Outlive the Leader 203

The Three Anchors of Leadership Continuity 203

Case Study 1: The BRAC Model, Bangladesh 205

Case Study 2: Nelson Mandela and the South African Transition 205

Building Leadership Multiplication into Your Impact Model 206

Avoiding the Founder's Trap 206

The Emotional Side of Letting Go 207

A Challenge to the Reader 208

Closing Thoughts 208

Chapter 6 – The Power of Cross-Sector Collaboration 211

Why Collaboration Is the Force Multiplier in Poverty Solutions
.... 211

The Collaboration Gap 211

Three Principles of High-Impact Collaboration 212

Case Study 1: Skills Future, Singapore 213

Case Study 2: Clean Water Coalitions in Kenya 213

Designing Your Own Cross-Sector Collaboration 214

The Leadership Skills Collaboration Requires 215

A Challenge to the Reader 215

Chapter 7 – Designing Solutions With, Not For, Communities
.... 217

Why Co-Creation Outperforms Top-Down Design 217

The Pitfalls of the "Parachute Approach" 218

Three Principles of Community Co-Creation 218

Case Study 1: Participatory Budgeting in Brazil 219

Case Study 2: Farmer-Led Irrigation in East Africa 219

A Leader's Guide to Co-Creation 220

The Mindset Shift Leaders Must Make 221

A Challenge to the Reader 221

Chapter 8 – Unlocking Economic Mobility Through Skills and Access 223

Why Economic Mobility Is the Real Poverty Breaker 223

The Three Levers of Economic Mobility 223

Case Study 1: Germany's Dual Vocational Training System 224

Case Study 2: Digital Skilling in Rural India 225

From Skills to Systems 225

The Leadership Role in Unlocking Access 226

Case Study 3: Peru's Artisan Export Network 227

Designing Your Own Economic Mobility Strategy 227

A Challenge to the Reader 228

Chapter 9 – Financing Change: Innovative Models for Sustainable Impact 229

Why Funding Models Make or Break Poverty Solutions 229

The Limitations of Traditional Funding 229

Four Innovative Models for Sustainable Impact 230

Case Study 1: Grameen Shakti, Bangladesh 231

Case Study 2: The Green Bond Movement 232

Designing a Sustainable Funding Strategy 232

Overcoming the Fear of "Profit" in Social Change 234

A Challenge to the Reader 234

Chapter 10 – Measuring What Matters Most 235

Why Measurement Is a Leadership Imperative 235

The Risks of Measuring the Wrong Things 235

Three Levels of Measurement for Poverty-Breaking Work 236

Case Study 1: The Multidimensional Poverty Index (MPI)
.... 237

**Case Study 2: Global Health Initiative's Outcome
Tracking** 237

How to Design a Measurement System That Works 238

From Data Collection to Data Culture 239

The Leadership Mindset for Measuring What Matters 239

A Challenge to the Reader 239

**Chapter 11 – Leveraging Technology Without Losing
Humanity** 241

Why Technology Is a Game-Changer — and a Risk 241

The Digital Divide: A Barrier to Inclusion 241

Three Principles for Human-Centered Tech in Poverty Solutions
.... 242

Case Study 1: Mobile Banking in Sub-Saharan Africa. 243

Case Study 2: Telemedicine in Rural Latin America ... 243

Making Technology Work for the Most Marginalized............244

Ethics in Tech-Driven Poverty Work 244

A Challenge to the Reader...245

Chapter 12 – Resilience in Leadership: Thriving in the Long Fight..246

Why Resilience Is a Strategic Advantage................................246

The Leadership Reality Check 246

Three Dimensions of Resilience...247

Case Study 1: Disaster Recovery Leadership in the Philippines..248

Case Study 2: The Long Game in Education Reform 248

Building Your Resilience Toolkit..248

The Mindset Shift from Endurance to Sustainability...............250

A Challenge to the Reader...250

Part III – Leader Journeys: Lessons from the Frontlines 251

Chapter 13 – From Violence to Vitality: The Medellín Transformation..252

A City at Rock Bottom...252

The Vision: Medellín, the Most Innovative City in the World 252

From Vision to Action: Integrated Urban Transformation . 253

The Impact: Numbers and Narratives.......................................254

Leadership Lessons from Medellín 255

Applying the Lessons Globally 256

A Challenge to the Reader...256

Chapter 14 – Microfinance and Women's Empowerment: The Grameen Story..258

The Problem No Bank Wanted to Solve 258

The Vision: Banking for the Poorest 258

From Vision to Action: The Grameen Model..........................259

The Impact: Beyond Numbers 260

Case Study: A Single Loan, A Ripple Effect 260

Leadership Lessons from Grameen 261

Global Adaptations of the Model 262

A Challenge to the Reader...262

Chapter 15 – Education as a Gateway: Pratham's India Model
.... 263

The Problem: School Attendance Without Learning...............263

The Vision: Every Child in School — and Learning Well......263

From Vision to Action: The Pratham Approach.......................264

The Impact: Scaling Simplicity 265

Case Study: The Village Learning Camp 265

Leadership Lessons from Pratham 266

Global Relevance 267

A Challenge to the Reader...267

Chapter 16 – Rebuilding Rwanda: Vision 2020 in Action 268

From National Trauma to National Determination..................268

The Vision: Middle-Income Status Within a Generation 268

From Vision to Action: The Strategic Blueprint.....................269

The Impact: Numbers and Narratives.....................................270

Case Study: The Coffee Sector Revival 271

Leadership Lessons from Vision 2020 271

Adapting the Lessons 272

A Challenge to the Reader...272

Chapter 17 – Local Innovation, Global Reach: The Kenya

Clean Water Coalition 273

The Problem: Water Scarcity Beyond Infrastructure.............. 273

The Vision: Reliable, Locally Managed Water for Every
Household 273

From Vision to Action: Building a Sustainable Water System
.... 274

The Impact: From Fetching to Flowing.................................. 275

Case Study: The Village of Makueni 275

Leadership Lessons from the Coalition 276

Global Applications... 276

A Challenge to the Reader... 277

**Chapter 18 – From Informal Settlements to Economic Hubs:
The Brazil Co-op Movement** 278

The Problem: Work Without Security..................................... 278

The Vision: Economic Dignity Through Self-Owned Enterprises
.... 278

From Vision to Action: Building the Co-op Network 279

The Impact: Ownership Changes Everything.......................... 280

Case Study: The Women's Catering Cooperative in Rio
.... 280

Leadership Lessons from the Co-op Movement...................... 281

Global Potential.. 281

A Challenge to the Reader... 282

Closing Part III – Leadership Beyond Borders....................... 282

Part IV – Your 284

Leadership Roadmap.. 284

Chapter 19 – Define Your Leadership Arena 285

Why Your Starting Point Matters.. 285

The Three Filters for Choosing Your Arena............................286

    Case Example: A CEO's Arena 286

    Step 1 – Map Your Sphere of Influence........................287

    Step 2 – Map Needs and Assets 287

    Step 3 – Choose Your Entry Point 288

    Avoid the "Everywhere at Once" Trap................................288

    A Challenge to the Reader..288

Chapter 20 – Craft Your Vision Statement............................290

    Why Vision Is Your Leadership North Star 290

    The Three Qualities of a Poverty-Breaking Vision 290

    Vision vs. Mission vs. Goals 291

    Case Study: Medellín's Vision...............................291

    Crafting Your Vision: A Step-by-Step Process.....................292

    Vision Statement Examples...292

    Common Vision Pitfalls to Avoid 293

    A Challenge to the Reader..293

Chapter 21 – Build Your First-Phase Action Plan 294

    Why a Vision Without a Plan Fails 294

    The 3 Elements of a First-Phase Plan................................294

    Case Study: First-Year Wins in a Youth Employment
    Initiative 295

    Step-by-Step: Building Your Plan......................................296

    Pro Tips for Early-Phase Leadership...................................297

    A Challenge to the Reader..297

Chapter 22 – Mobilize Your Allies.......................................298

    Why Allies Multiply Your Impact.......................................298

    The 3 Types of Allies You Need 298

Case Study: The Clean Water Coalition's Ally Map...... 299

Step-by-Step: Mobilizing Your Allies..................................... 300

Tips for Keeping Allies Engaged 300

A Challenge to the Reader.. 301

Chapter 23 – Secure Sustainable Resources........................... 302

Why Sustainability Beats Survival... 302

The 4 Resource Streams Every Leader Should Consider 302

Case Study: Financing a Rural Skills Hub 303

Step-by-Step: Building Your Sustainable Resource Plan 304

Overcoming Common Funding Fears 305

A Challenge to the Reader.. 305

Chapter 24 – Measure, Adapt, and Scale 306

Why Tracking and Adapting Are Non-Negotiable.................. 306

The Three-Part Cycle of Continuous Improvement 306

Case Study: Scaling a Digital Literacy Program 307

Step-by-Step: Your Measure–Adapt–Scale Process................ 308

Scaling Pitfalls to Avoid.. 308

A Challenge to the Reader.. 309

Chapter 25 – Lead for the Long Game...................................... 310

Why the Long Game Matters.. 310

The Three Foundations of Long-Term Leadership................... 310

Case Study: A Housing Nonprofit's Smooth Transition311

Building Resilience Into Your Leadership 312

Leaving a Legacy That Lasts.. 312

A Challenge to the Reader..313

Part IV – Your Leadership Roadmap You now have............313

The Poverty-Breaking Leader's Oath 315

Why This Oath Matters 315

The Oath 316

Looking Ahead..318

Epilogue – From Vision to Impact: A Final Call to Lead Boldly
.... 319

The Journey Revisited 319

Why Leaders Must Act Now 319

Vision → Action → Impact: The Leadership Blueprint 320

A Call to Bold Leadership 321

The Final Word 321

DTD's Leadership Playbook & Blueprint 323

Introducing DTD's Leadership Playbook & Blueprint..........324

DTD's Leadership Playbook & Blueprint..............................326

A Guide for Leaders and Aspiring Leaders to Break the Cycle of Poverty 326

I. The Four Pillars of Leadership...326

II. The Three Phases of the Blueprint...................................326

Phase 2: Action – Building the Bridge Between Vision and Reality..326

Phase 3: Impact – Phase 1: Vision – Seeing Beyond the Present..327

• **Define the Future**: Articulate a vivid picture of prosperity for your community or organization. 327

• **Identify Barriers**: Pinpoint systemic, cultural, or economic blocks that perpetuate poverty. 327

• **Set Bold Goals**: Establish specific, measurable outcomes (e.g., increase college enrollment by 25% in 5 years) 327

Leadership Tool: The **Vision Map** – a one-page document
outlining what success looks like in 5, 10, and 20 years 328

Measuring What Matters Most 328

III. The Leadership Pathways in Action 328

IV. Action Checkpoints for Leaders 329

V. The Playbook Promise 329

Introduction – The Foundation of From Poverty to Prosperity

Before *From Poverty to Prosperity* could be written, there was a body of work that laid the cornerstone. That body of work was a collection of focused, practical guides—each one tackling a distinct dimension of poverty and pointing toward actionable solutions.

Together, these 14 works became a **blueprint of pathways**. Each title represented a solution area, and together they outlined a holistic vision for how leaders, communities, and institutions could break cycles of disadvantage.

The Fourteen Pathways to Breaking Poverty

1. **Breaking the Cycle of Poverty Through Innate Skillset Development** – Unlocking natural talent and capability that poverty often obscures.
2. **Breaking the Cycle of Poverty Through Youth Development Programs** – Positioning young people as active participants in building their futures.

3. **Breaking the Cycle of Poverty Through Advocacy & Leadership** – Giving communities the voice and influence to shape policies and systems.

4. **Breaking the Cycle of Poverty Through Leadership Training & Development** – Equipping leaders at every level with the tools to

5.　dismantle entrenched barriers.

6. **Breaking the Cycle of Poverty Through College Exploration & Development** – Expanding horizons and making higher education an accessible pathway to mobility.

7. **Breaking the Cycle of Poverty Through Career Readiness Development** – Preparing individuals not just for jobs, but for careers that sustain growth.

8. **Breaking the Cycle of Poverty Through Business Education & Development** – Transforming entrepreneurs into employers, innovators, and wealth creators.

9. **Breaking the Cycle of Poverty Through Workforce Development Education** – Aligning skills training with the evolving demands of the global economy.

10. **Breaking the Cycle of Poverty Through Health & Wellness** – Recognizing health as the foundation for productivity, stability, and longevity.

11. **Breaking the Cycle of Poverty Through Parental Program Development** – Empowering parents to create stability and opportunity for the next generation.

12. **Breaking the Cycle of Poverty Through Building & Sustaining Community Relationships** – Harnessing trust and collaboration as economic

multipliers.

13. **Breaking the Cycle of Poverty Through Sports, Education & Leadership** – Leveraging athletics as a platform for discipline, education, and opportunity.

14. **Breaking the Cycle of Poverty Through Civic Engagement and Leadership** – Mobilizing communities to influence decisions and policies.

15. **Breaking the Cycle of Poverty Through Financial Wealth Development** – Turning income gains into lasting generational assets.

From Pathways to Framework

Each of these titles served as a **standalone solution pathway**. They answered the question: *What can we do?*

But taken together, they also revealed something larger: the need for a **comprehensive leadership framework** to weave them into a coherent, scalable approach.

That is where *From Poverty to Prosperity* begins— integrating all fourteen pathways into the **Vision → Action → Impact** model:

- **Vision** defines the future we believe is possible.
- **Action** implements targeted strategies across these

pathways.

- **Impact** ensures that change is measurable, sustainable, and generational.

Why This Book Is the Next Step

From Poverty to Prosperity builds on the foundation of these fourteen works by moving beyond **individual solutions** to a **unified framework of leadership**. It equips leaders to integrate, scale, and sustain these pathways so that poverty is not just managed, but broken—permanently.

This introduction stands as a bridge: honoring the groundwork laid in the *Breaking the Cycle* series while inviting readers into the next stage—a leadership journey designed to move vision into action, and action into lasting impact.

Before we can fully appreciate the framework presented in *From Poverty to Prosperity*, it is important to recognize the foundation upon which it stands. This book is not a starting point—it is the continuation of a journey. The insights, strategies, and solutions you will encounter here are built on years of research, practice, and publication. Each earlier work explored a specific pathway for breaking the cycle of poverty, and together they created a library of solutions that paved the way for this larger vision. What follows is a brief overview of those works, which form both the context and the catalyst for the book you now hold.

Chapter 1 – The Leadership Mandate

Why Leadership Matters More Than Ever

Every movement for lasting change has one thing in common—leaders who refuse to accept the status quo. Poverty will not be solved by policies alone, nor will it be erased by charity without strategy. It will be broken by individuals and organizations willing to lead with courage, creativity, and consistency.

Leadership is not reserved for CEOs, politicians, or public figures. In the fight against poverty, leadership can—and must—exist at every level: in classrooms, in community centers, in small businesses, in city halls, and in living rooms. The Leadership Mandate is the recognition that every person who has influence over decisions, resources, or people has a role to play.

The Difference Between Leadership and Position

Titles do not make leaders—impact does.
 Too often, leadership is mistaken for positional authority, but breaking the cycle of poverty requires leaders who are defined not

by where they sit on an organizational chart, but by the changes they create.

True leadership in this space requires:

- **Vision** – seeing beyond immediate needs to long-term transformation.
- **Empathy** – understanding the lived experiences of those you serve.
- **Resolve** – staying committed even when solutions take years to bear fruit.
- **Adaptability** – knowing when to innovate, when to collaborate, and when to advocate.

The Moral and Economic Imperative

Fighting poverty is not just an act of compassion—it's an investment in our collective future. Communities weighed down by poverty face higher crime rates, lower educational outcomes, and reduced economic productivity. Breaking that cycle lifts everyone, fueling economic growth, expanding talent pipelines, and creating more stable societies.

When leaders take action against poverty, they are not just helping individuals—they are strengthening the very systems that underpin prosperity. That is why the Leadership Mandate is not optional. If you have the ability to lead, you have the responsibility to lead.

Your Role in the Mandate

As you read this book, I want you to see yourself not just as a consumer of ideas, but as an active participant in a global movement. Whether your influence spans a team of five or a city of five million, you have the capacity to be a poverty breaker.

In the coming chapters, you will see how to apply the **Vision to Action to Impact** framework in ways that fit your sphere of influence, your resources, and your mission. You will learn how to identify opportunities, mobilize resources, and measure results—not just for short-term wins, but for long-term, generational change.

The Leadership Mandate is clear: the power to break poverty exists in the decisions we make, the actions we take, and the partnerships we build. The question is not *whether* we can do it—it's *whether we will choose to*.

Chapter 2 – Breaking Limiting Beliefs

The Invisible Walls Around Us

Some of the strongest barriers to prosperity are not physical—they are mental.

They live in the unspoken assumptions we hold about ourselves, our communities, and what is possible. These *limiting beliefs* act like invisible walls, keeping people from pursuing opportunities even when the door is open.

For those living in poverty, limiting beliefs can be deeply ingrained:

- *"People like me don't get ahead."*
- *"Education is for others, not for me."*
- *"No matter what I do, nothing will change."*

But limiting beliefs are not unique to those in poverty. Leaders, too, can fall victim to them:

- *"The problem is too big to solve."*
- *"Change takes generations—there's no point in trying now."*
- *"It's not my responsibility."*

The first step toward breaking the cycle of poverty is dismantling these mental barriers.

How Limiting Beliefs Take Root

Limiting beliefs rarely start with one event; they grow from repeated experiences, often reinforced by environment and culture.

When people see more examples of failure than success, more barriers than breakthroughs, they internalize the message that their future is already decided.

Leaders must recognize that breaking poverty's grip is not just about providing resources—it's about rewriting narratives.

Replacing Limiting Beliefs with Empowering Truths

Beliefs can be challenged and replaced. Leaders can help communities shift their mindset by:

- **Modeling success** – showcasing relatable role models who have overcome similar challenges.
- **Creating early wins** – helping individuals experience achievable successes that build confidence.

- **Speaking possibility** – intentionally using language that emphasizes opportunity, capability, and choice.
- **Connecting to purpose** – reminding people of their unique value and potential.

Your Role as a Belief-Breaker

As a leader, you are both a strategist and a storyteller. You don't just provide tools—you show people why they should believe they can use them. You set the tone in meetings, classrooms, boardrooms, and town halls.

Every time you communicate, you either reinforce limitations or open the door to possibility. That is why *breaking limiting beliefs is leadership work.*

From Mindset Shift to Movement

When limiting beliefs are challenged on a personal level, change begins. But when they are challenged collectively—within a school, a workplace, a community—momentum builds. People begin to see themselves differently, and with that new identity, they make new choices.

Those choices lead to action.
 Action leads to impact.
 And impact fuels a new cycle—one of possibility and progress instead of poverty.

In the next chapter, we will explore how to channel this new mindset into **innate skillset development**—the process of uncovering and strengthening the talents that will carry people toward lasting prosperity.

Chapter 3 – Innate Skillset Development

Why Skills Matter More Than Resources Alone

When a person's mindset changes, the door to possibility opens—but walking through that door requires skill. Without the ability to apply their new belief in themselves to practical, income-generating, and problem-solving actions, even the most motivated individuals can stall.

This is why skillset development is the natural next step after breaking limiting beliefs. Leaders who want to break the cycle of poverty must invest in helping people uncover and grow the abilities they already possess, and then align those abilities with market needs and opportunities.

The Power of Innate Skills

Innate skills are talents and capabilities a person already has—often unnoticed or undervalued. These could be:

- Natural problem-solving abilities.
- Communication and relationship-building skills.
- Creativity in art, design, or innovation.

- Technical abilities learned informally (e.g., mechanics, carpentry, digital literacy).

- Leadership potential demonstrated in informal community roles.

Many times, these skills are overshadowed by the urgency of survival. Leaders must help surface them, refine them, and connect them to opportunities.

From Hidden Talent to Marketable Strength

The process of turning innate skill into prosperity can be broken into three stages:

1. **Discovery** – Helping individuals identify what they do naturally well. This can be through workshops, mentorship, or simple observation.

2. **Development** – Providing targeted training to refine and expand those skills into competencies that meet industry or community needs.

3. **Deployment** – Creating pathways for individuals to use their skills in employment, entrepreneurship, or leadership roles.

Why Leaders Must Lead This Process

In communities facing poverty, there is often no formal system to guide people from raw talent to opportunity. Leaders—whether in business, education, or nonprofit sectors—must create these systems.

That can mean:

- Partnering with local businesses to design apprenticeship programs.
- Creating community skill-mapping projects to identify untapped talent.
- Offering training that blends technical skills with soft skills like teamwork, problem-solving, and communication.
- Connecting skill development to real economic opportunities rather than training for training's sake.

The Ripple Effect of Skill Development

When one person gains a marketable skill, the impact extends far beyond them. They can:

- Earn higher wages and build financial stability.

- Serve as a role model to others in their family or community.

- Contribute to local economies as both employees and entrepreneurs.

This is how skillset development moves from individual empowerment to collective prosperity—and why it is a core pillar of the **Vision to Action to Impact** framework.

Looking Ahead

With the right mindset and skillset in place, individuals and communities are ready to engage with broader systems of opportunity. In the next chapter, we will explore how **youth development as a cornerstone** can set these processes in motion earlier, preventing cycles of poverty from taking root in the first place.

Chapter 4 – Youth Development as the Cornerstone

Why Start with Youth?

If we want to break the cycle of poverty, we must begin before it takes hold. Youth development is not simply a programmatic choice—it's a strategic investment. By equipping young people early with the skills, confidence, and networks they need, we give them a head start toward prosperity and drastically reduce the likelihood they will remain trapped in the conditions they were born into.

Youth are adaptable, full of potential, and naturally positioned to influence their peers. When we nurture their leadership abilities, creativity, and problem-solving skills early, we plant seeds that will grow into stronger communities for decades to come.

The Cost of Neglect

When youth development is ignored or underfunded, the consequences ripple outward:

- Higher dropout rates.

- Increased unemployment among young adults.
- Greater vulnerability to crime, exploitation, and systemic cycles of poverty.
- Lost opportunities for innovation and leadership.

These are not just personal losses—they are societal losses, draining communities of future contributors, innovators, and changemakers.

Building Effective Youth Development Programs

Successful youth development goes beyond after-school activities. It requires intentional, structured programming that addresses multiple dimensions of growth:

1. **Academic Support** – Tutoring, STEM engagement, literacy programs, and college readiness initiatives.
2. **Skill Development** – Technical, vocational, and entrepreneurial training tied to real-world opportunities.
3. **Leadership Training** – Public speaking, civic engagement, decision-making, and conflict resolution.
4. **Mentorship** – Consistent guidance from trusted adults who model positive behavior and open doors to new experiences.

5. **Community Involvement** – Opportunities for youth to contribute to local projects, strengthening their sense of belonging and responsibility.

The Leadership Role in Youth Development

As leaders, we cannot simply delegate youth development to schools or nonprofits—it must be embedded into business, government, and community strategies. That means:

- Partnering with schools to integrate career readiness into curricula.
- Offering internships and apprenticeships that connect learning to earning.
- Funding programs that make leadership training accessible to all youth, not just the privileged few.
- Advocating for policy changes that prioritize early investment in young people.

Case Example: From Youth Leader to Community Leader

One of the most powerful outcomes of youth development programs is seeing participants return as adult leaders. A teenager mentored in high school may return years later as a business owner, educator, or elected official—ready to invest back into the next generation. This creates a **virtuous cycle** that reinforces prosperity over time.

A Foundation for Everything Else

Youth development is not a single project—it is the bedrock upon which all other poverty-breaking strategies rest. If we build strong, confident, skilled young people, they will become the leaders who carry forward the **Vision to Action to Impact** framework in ways we cannot yet imagine.

Chapter 5 – Advocacy and Civic Leadership

Why Advocacy Matters in the Fight Against Poverty

Programs, skills training, and community initiatives are powerful—but without systemic change, their impact is limited. Poverty is not sustained only by a lack of resources; it is reinforced by policies, institutional practices, and public priorities that either create opportunity or restrict it. Advocacy is how we ensure the systems themselves work for people, not against them.

Civic leadership means stepping beyond individual or organizational boundaries to influence laws, policies, and cultural norms. It's about using your voice, your platform, and your networks to create the conditions where prosperity is possible for everyone.

The Misunderstanding About Advocacy

Too often, advocacy is seen as political in the narrow sense—limited to rallies, speeches, or lobbying lawmakers. While these are valuable tools, advocacy is far broader. It happens every time you:

- Speak up for underrepresented voices in decision-making spaces.
- Push for funding that directly benefits underserved communities.
- Use data and storytelling to shift public perception on poverty issues.
- Form coalitions that amplify community needs.

Advocacy is not just about protest—it is about persistent, strategic action that turns awareness into policy and policy into impact.

Building Civic Leaders from the Ground Up

Civic leadership isn't reserved for elected officials. It belongs to:

- Business leaders who influence economic priorities.
- Educators who shape how students see their role in society.
- Faith leaders who mobilize congregations to meet community needs.
- Youth who organize peers around causes that matter to them.

To build civic leaders, we must:

1. **Educate** – Teach how government, policy, and civic processes work.
2. **Empower** – Provide tools and platforms for people to engage meaningfully.
3. **Equip** – Offer mentorship and resources that prepare leaders to navigate the challenges of public influence.

The Leader's Role in Advocacy

If you have influence, you have a responsibility to use it for the greater good. Leaders can:

- Serve on advisory boards or task forces that shape community policy.
- Advocate for equitable hiring, training, and wage policies within their organizations.
- Collaborate with the local government to create poverty-focused development initiatives.
- Use media platforms to keep the conversation on poverty visible and urgent.

From Voice to Victory

Advocacy is not about winning every battle—it's about persistence. Policy change can be slow, but consistent pressure and strategic alliances can yield lasting results. The victories may be incremental, but over time they reshape the landscape in which communities operate.

Looking Ahead

Advocacy and civic leadership ensure that the progress we make through programs and partnerships is protected, expanded, and sustained. In the next chapter, we will turn our focus inward, exploring **Leadership Training & Development**—because the fight against poverty needs not just more leaders, but better-prepared leaders, at every level.

Chapter 6 – Leadership Training & Development

Why Leadership Development Is Essential to Ending Poverty

Leaders are the multipliers of change. A single committed leader can influence hundreds—or even thousands—of lives through decisions, vision, and the ability to mobilize resources. But leadership is not an inborn trait reserved for a few; it is a skill set that can be learned, honed, and passed on.

If we are serious about breaking the cycle of poverty, we must not only develop programs for communities—we must develop the people who will lead those programs, initiatives, and movements. Leadership training is the investment that ensures our strategies endure beyond any one person, organization, or funding cycle.

The Gap in Leadership Preparedness

In many communities, especially those facing systemic poverty, there is no intentional pathway for developing leaders. Talented individuals often rise to informal leadership roles without formal training in:

- Strategic planning
- Resource management
- Conflict resolution
- Public communication
- Data-driven decision-making

Without these skills, leaders can burn out quickly, lose influence, or be unable to scale their impact. Training closes this gap, turning potential into sustained performance.

Core Elements of Effective Leadership Training

Leadership development should be practical, inclusive, and results-oriented. Effective programs often include:

1. **Self-Leadership** – Building self-awareness, resilience, and the discipline to lead by example.
2. **Strategic Thinking** – Learning to assess needs, prioritize initiatives, and allocate resources effectively.
3. **Communication Skills** – Mastering public speaking, persuasive writing, and active listening.
4. **Team Building & Management** – Creating high-performing teams through trust, clarity, and accountability.

5. **Change Management** – Guiding individuals and organizations through transitions without losing momentum.
6. **Ethics & Integrity** – Leading with transparency, fairness, and a long-term vision for the common good.

Creating a Leadership Pipeline

One of the most powerful legacies a leader can leave is a **pipeline of prepared successors**. This means:

- Identifying emerging leaders early.
- Providing mentorship and hands-on leadership opportunities.
- Offering tiered training so leaders grow at every stage of their journey.
- Encouraging cross-sector collaboration so leaders understand different perspectives.

This pipeline approach ensures leadership is not concentrated in a few hands, but distributed across a network of capable change agents.

Case in Point

I have seen communities where leadership development

changed the entire trajectory of a neighborhood. When multiple leaders emerge—trained, connected, and empowered—they spark simultaneous change in education, business, policy, and community health. It's no longer one voice calling for progress—it's a chorus.

From Training to Transformation

Leadership training is not an academic exercise; it is preparation for the front lines of real-world change. It equips leaders to navigate obstacles, inspire others, and sustain the fight against poverty over the long term.

In the next chapter, we will explore **Education Pathways: From College to Career**—the bridge that ensures learning leads to opportunity, and opportunity leads to lasting prosperity.

Chapter 7 – Education Pathways: From College to Career

Why Education Must Lead to Opportunity

Education is often called the great equalizer—but only when it is paired with clear, accessible pathways to real-world opportunities. Far too often, students—especially in underserved communities—complete schooling without a roadmap for how to translate their learning into a meaningful career. The result? Degrees without direction, skills without application, and dreams that stall before they take flight.

A true education pathway bridges the gap between the classroom and the workplace, ensuring that every graduate has both the knowledge and the navigational tools to thrive.

The Disconnect Between Education and Employment

Many young people enter higher education believing it guarantees success, only to graduate into unemployment or underemployment. This disconnect stems from:

- Lack of career exploration during high school.

- Education programs that do not align with current or emerging job markets.
- Insufficient mentoring and networking opportunities.
- Limited access to internships or work-based learning.

Without intentional bridges, students are left to navigate the transition from college to career on their own—and too many fall through the cracks.

Building Effective Education-to-Career Pipelines

To break the cycle of poverty, education pathways must be strategic, practical, and personalized. Leaders can strengthen these pipelines by:

1. **Early Career Exposure** – Integrating career exploration into middle and high school curricula.
2. **College Readiness Programs** – Providing students with academic preparation, financial literacy, and time management skills before they enter higher education.
3. **Industry-Aligned Curricula** – Partnering with businesses to ensure training matches workforce needs.
4. **Internships & Apprenticeships** – Giving students hands-on experience and professional connections.

5. **Mentorship Networks** – Connecting students with professionals in their chosen fields for guidance and support.

6. **Soft Skills Development** – Teaching communication, teamwork, adaptability, and leadership alongside technical knowledge.

The Role of Leaders in Strengthening Pathways

Whether in education, business, or community leadership, we can all play a role in ensuring education leads to opportunity. This might include:

- Sponsoring scholarships for underrepresented students.
- Offering workplace tours or shadowing experiences.
- Collaborating with local colleges to shape curriculum.
- Hosting career fairs focused on industries with growth potential.

When leaders intentionally connect education to career readiness, they help students see not just where they are going, but *how* to get there.

A Vision for Generational Change

When students graduate with a clear path to stable, fulfilling careers, they break personal cycles of poverty and set a new standard for the next generation. Their children grow up in homes where higher education and career achievement are not exceptions—they are expectations.

Looking Ahead

Education pathways are critical, but they are only one part of the economic puzzle. In the next chapter, we will explore **Business Education & Entrepreneurship**—a strategy that not only creates jobs but empowers people to own the means of their prosperity.

Chapter 8 – Business Education & Entrepreneurship

From Employee to Employer: Expanding the Vision

For generations, the path to economic security was framed almost exclusively around finding a good job. But in communities where poverty persists, job opportunities are often scarce or unstable. Business education and entrepreneurship provide an alternative—and sometimes more powerful—path to prosperity: creating the opportunities that others can access.

Teaching people how to start, grow, and sustain businesses equips them not only to earn income for themselves but to contribute to the economic vitality of their communities.

The Power of Business Literacy

Business literacy is more than knowing how to balance a budget or write a business plan. It's about understanding:

- **How money moves** within a business and across an economy.

- **How to identify unmet needs** and turn them into products or services.
- **How to manage risk** while pursuing growth.
- **How to scale** from a one-person operation to a sustainable enterprise.

Without these skills, even the most innovative ideas can fail before they take root.

Entrepreneurship as a Poverty Breaker

Entrepreneurship offers unique advantages in the fight against poverty:

1. **Ownership** – Building assets that can be passed on to future generations.
2. **Job Creation** – Providing employment opportunities for others in the community.
3. **Local Investment** – Keeping profits circulating within the community rather than flowing out.
4. **Innovation** – Solving local problems with local solutions.

Integrating Business Education into Community Development

Leaders can expand entrepreneurial capacity by:

- Hosting **business bootcamps** that cover planning, financing, marketing, and operations.
- Partnering with **microfinance institutions** to provide access to startup capital.
- Creating **incubators or co-working spaces** that lower the cost of launching a business.
- Connecting entrepreneurs to **mentors** who can help them avoid common pitfalls.
- Encouraging **youth entrepreneurship programs** to spark early interest and skills.

A Culture of Possibility

In communities where traditional employment opportunities are limited, entrepreneurship sends a powerful message: you are not limited to the jobs available—you can create your own. This cultural shift is critical. When people see their neighbors successfully running businesses, they begin to believe it's possible for themselves.

From Small Businesses to Economic Engines

A single small business may employ only a handful of people, but when many small businesses thrive, they collectively form a resilient economic base. Over time, these enterprises can attract investment, strengthen local supply chains, and elevate the standard of living for entire neighborhoods.

Looking Ahead

Entrepreneurship is a powerful driver of prosperity, but it works best alongside strong workforce systems that prepare people for employment in growing industries. In the next chapter, we will explore **Workforce Development & Employment Pathways**—how to align skills, training, and job opportunities to create stable, long-term income streams.

Chapter 9 – Workforce Development & Employment Pathways

Why Workforce Development Matters

While entrepreneurship creates powerful opportunities for ownership, the majority of people will still rely on employment as their primary source of income. In communities where poverty is entrenched, workforce development is not simply about filling jobs—it's about equipping people with the skills, confidence, and networks to secure and sustain meaningful work.

When designed intentionally, workforce development programs do more than prepare people for a paycheck—they prepare them for long-term career growth and financial stability.

The Workforce Readiness Gap

Many employers struggle to fill positions not because jobs don't exist, but because candidates lack the right mix of technical and soft skills. This gap can be traced to:

- Outdated or irrelevant training programs.

- Lack of alignment between education and industry needs.
- Insufficient exposure to career possibilities.
- Limited access to professional networks.

Without intervention, this gap perpetuates cycles of underemployment and financial insecurity.

Core Components of Effective Workforce Development

A strong workforce development system integrates:

1. **Skills Assessment** – Understanding current abilities and matching them to market demands.
2. **Industry-Specific Training** – Providing targeted instruction in sectors with growth potential.
3. **Soft Skills Development** – Teaching professionalism, communication, problem-solving, and adaptability.
4. **Hands-On Experience** – Offering internships, apprenticeships, and on-the-job training.
5. **Career Navigation Support** – Guiding individuals through resume building, job searches, and interviews.
6. **Retention & Advancement Support** – Offering mentorship and upskilling opportunities after initial

employment.

The Leader's Role in Workforce Pathways

Leaders across sectors can strengthen workforce systems by:

- Partnering with local employers to ensure training programs match hiring needs.
- Advocating for funding and policies that expand workforce training access.
- Supporting wraparound services such as childcare, transportation, and counseling that remove employment barriers.
- Encouraging businesses to hire from within the community and invest in employee development.

Case Example: Aligning Skills with Opportunity

In cities where workforce training is closely tied to economic development planning, job seekers are equipped with skills for industries that are actively hiring—such as healthcare, renewable energy, technology, and skilled trades. This alignment ensures that training investments pay off quickly, both for the individual and the local economy.

From Job Placement to Career Growth

True poverty-breaking employment pathways focus not just on getting people into jobs, but on helping them *grow* in those jobs—through promotions, further education, and leadership opportunities. Stability turns into upward mobility when continuous learning and advancement are prioritized.

Looking Ahead

Workforce development is essential for financial stability, but to build generational wealth, we must go further. In the next chapter, we will explore **Financial Wealth Development**—how to move beyond income to create assets, investments, and security that last for decades.

Chapter 10 – Financial Wealth Development

From Earning to Building

Employment and entrepreneurship generate income, but income alone does not create lasting financial security. True prosperity comes from transforming earnings into assets—resources that grow in value over time, can be passed down, and provide stability regardless of short-term economic changes.

For many, especially in communities affected by poverty, financial wealth is a foreign concept. Too often, the focus is on *making ends meet*, not *making money work*. Financial wealth development changes this mindset and equips people with the tools to move from survival to stability, and from stability to abundance.

Why Financial Wealth Matters

Wealth is more than money in the bank. It's the freedom to make choices, the security to weather challenges, and the power to invest in future opportunities. Financial wealth allows individuals and families to:

- Break free from the paycheck-to-paycheck cycle.
- Provide educational opportunities for their children.
- Start businesses or invest in community growth.
- Retire without financial anxiety.

Core Elements of Wealth Development

1. **Financial Literacy** – Understanding budgeting, debt management, credit, and interest.
2. **Savings Discipline** – Building emergency funds and long-term savings habits.
3. **Investment Knowledge** – Learning the basics of stocks, bonds, mutual funds, and retirement accounts.
4. **Asset Ownership** – Acquiring property, real estate, or other appreciating assets.
5. **Insurance & Protection** – Safeguarding against financial loss through health, life, and property insurance.
6. **Estate Planning** – Creating wills, trusts, and succession plans to transfer wealth to future generations.

Breaking Cultural and Systemic Barriers

In many underserved communities, systemic barriers—such as predatory lending, lack of access to capital, and discriminatory housing policies—have historically blocked wealth accumulation. Leaders must advocate for equitable access to banking, investment opportunities, and home ownership, while also providing education that empowers individuals to make informed financial choices.

Teaching Wealth as a Community Value

Wealth development is not just an individual pursuit—it's a community strategy. When more households hold assets, communities gain:

- Increased local investment.
- Stronger tax bases for schools and infrastructure.
- Greater resilience against economic downturns.

By normalizing conversations about wealth in schools, community centers, and faith institutions, leaders can help dismantle the belief that wealth is "for other people" and make it a shared goal.

From Survival to Legacy

Financial wealth development is about creating **legacy**. It is ensuring that the next generation starts further ahead than the last. When communities learn not just how to earn but how to grow and protect wealth, the cycle of poverty can be replaced with a cycle of opportunity and abundance.

Looking Ahead

Financial security provides the foundation for health, stability, and personal growth. In the next chapter, we will explore **Health & Wellness as a Prosperity Driver**— because no amount of income or wealth can replace the value of physical, mental, and emotional well-being in building a thriving life.

Chapter 11 – Health & Wellness as a Prosperity Driver

Why Health Is Wealth

You can have skills, education, and income—but without good health, sustaining prosperity becomes almost impossible. Chronic illness, untreated mental health challenges, and preventable diseases can strip away savings, limit career opportunities, and diminish quality of life.

For communities in poverty, the health gap is stark. Limited access to nutritious food, safe housing, clean environments, and affordable healthcare compounds the challenges of economic advancement. To truly break the cycle of poverty, we must see health and wellness not as a luxury, but as a critical driver of prosperity.

The Poverty–Health Connection

Poverty and poor health reinforce each other:

- **Limited healthcare access** leads to untreated conditions that affect work and daily life.
- **Stress and anxiety** from financial strain contribute to

chronic illness.

- **Food insecurity** results in poor nutrition and related health issues.
- **Unsafe environments** increase risk of injury and disease.

Breaking this cycle requires integrated solutions that address both economic and health challenges simultaneously.

Core Areas of Wellness for Lasting Prosperity

1. **Physical Health** – Access to preventative care, regular check-ups, and treatment for chronic conditions.
2. **Mental Health** – Support for stress management, counseling, and destigmatizing mental health conversations.
3. **Nutrition** – Education on healthy eating, coupled with affordable, accessible food options.
4. **Fitness & Activity** – Community-based programs that promote movement, recreation, and overall vitality.
5. **Work–Life Balance** – Policies and practices that allow individuals to sustain productivity without burnout.

The Role of Leaders in Promoting Wellness

Leaders in every sector can play a role in driving health equity by:

- Partnering with healthcare providers to bring services into underserved neighborhoods.
- Supporting workplace wellness programs that encourage healthy habits.
- Advocating for policy changes that expand access to affordable healthcare.
- Funding or organizing community fitness and nutrition initiatives.

The Economic Impact of Wellness

Healthy individuals are more productive, have fewer work absences, and are better able to pursue education and career growth. Communities with strong health systems attract business investment, reduce public healthcare costs, and build a stronger workforce.

From Surviving to Thriving

Health is not just the absence of illness—it's the presence of vitality. When people are physically strong, mentally resilient, and emotionally balanced, they can fully engage in the opportunities created by education, workforce development, and entrepreneurship.

Looking Ahead

Wellness is deeply tied to the stability of the family unit. In the next chapter, we will explore **Parental Program Development**—how equipping parents with skills, resources, and support systems ensures that children grow up in environments where prosperity is possible.

Chapter 12 – Parental Program Development

Why Parents Are the Cornerstone of Prosperity

When parents thrive, children thrive.

The home environment shapes a child's sense of security, ambition, and belief in what's possible. Parents are a child's first teachers, role models, and advocates. Yet in communities impacted by poverty, parents often face overwhelming challenges—economic stress, limited access to resources, and a lack of support systems—that make it harder to provide stability and opportunity for their children.

Parental program development recognizes that breaking the cycle of poverty requires equipping parents with the tools, knowledge, and confidence to lead their families toward prosperity.

The Link Between Parenting and Poverty Outcomes

Children raised in homes with consistent structure, emotional support, and access to learning resources are far more likely to succeed academically, socially, and economically.

Conversely, households where parents are overworked, under-resourced, or unsupported often pass down cycles of instability.

Strong parental programs can help address:

- Limited financial literacy.
- Lack of access to childcare or quality early education.
- Stress and burnout affecting parental engagement.
- Gaps in parenting skills due to generational poverty.

Core Components of Effective Parental Programs

1. **Parent Education** – Classes on child development, communication, discipline, and academic support.
2. **Economic Empowerment** – Job training, entrepreneurship guidance, and financial literacy for parents.
3. **Health & Wellness Support** – Counseling, healthcare access, and stress management resources.
4. **Community Connection** – Networking opportunities with other parents for mutual support.
5. **Resource Navigation** – Guidance on accessing local programs, grants, and public benefits.

The Role of Leaders in Supporting Parents

Leaders—whether in business, education, faith, or community organizations—can strengthen parental programs by:

- Partnering with schools to provide evening or weekend classes for parents.
- Offering family-inclusive workplace benefits like flexible scheduling and childcare support.
- Creating mentorship programs that connect experienced parents with those who are struggling.
- Advocating for public policies that improve access to affordable childcare and parental leave.

Case Example: Whole-Family Impact

In communities where parental programs have been implemented, schools report higher student attendance and performance, while parents experience increased confidence and stability. These programs create a **ripple effect**—strengthening families, which in turn strengthens communities.

From Parent Support to Generational Change

When parents have the resources and skills they need, they

can break cycles of poverty within their own families. The habits, values, and stability they provide become a legacy for their children, shifting the trajectory for future generations.

Looking Ahead

Strong families are the foundation of strong communities. In the next chapter, we will explore **Sports, Education & Leadership**—how combining athletics with education and leadership training can inspire young people and build essential life skills.

Chapter 13 – Sports, Education & Leadership

More Than a Game

Sports have long been a unifying force in communities. They inspire passion, teamwork, and resilience. But when intentionally integrated with education and leadership development, sports become far more than physical competition—they become a powerful tool for breaking the cycle of poverty.

For many young people, sports provide structure, mentorship, and a sense of belonging that might otherwise be missing. They can open doors to scholarships, career opportunities, and personal growth, while also reinforcing academic commitment and leadership values.

Why Sports Are a Unique Opportunity

Sports naturally teach lessons essential for succcss in life and business:

- Discipline and time management.
- Goal setting and perseverance.
- Collaboration and communication.

- Handling both success and failure with integrity.

When paired with education and leadership programs, these lessons translate directly into improved school performance, better decision-making, and stronger leadership capacity.

The Risk Without Integration

While sports can be transformative, the benefits often fade if they're not connected to broader life skills and academic goals. Without intentional integration:

- Athletes may neglect academics, limiting future opportunities.
- Physical talent may overshadow the need for personal development.
- The end of an athletic career can leave young people without direction.

This is why sports programs must be designed to reinforce— not replace—academic achievement and leadership growth.

Building Integrated Sports–Education– Leadership Programs

1. **Academic Accountability** – Linking participation to classroom performance and tutoring support.
2. **Leadership Curriculum** – Embedding leadership

workshops into sports schedules.

3. **Mentorship** – Connecting athletes with coaches, alumni, and community leaders who model positive life choices.

4. **Career Exposure** – Showing that sports careers go beyond being an athlete, including coaching, sports medicine, management, and media.

5. **Community Engagement** – Involving teams in service projects to build civic responsibility.

The Role of Leaders in Leveraging Sports for Change

Leaders can:

- Partner with schools and sports leagues to embed educational and leadership goals into athletic programs.
- Provide funding for academic support services tied to sports participation.
- Advocate for equal access to sports for girls and underrepresented youth.
- Create post-sports career planning resources for young athletes.

Case Example: Teamwork Beyond the Field

In communities where sports are tied to leadership development, young athletes often go on to excel in academics, win scholarships, and become community leaders. The teamwork and discipline learned on the field translate directly into boardrooms, classrooms, and civic life.

From the Field to the Future

Sports can be the spark—but education and leadership are the fuel that keeps young people moving forward. When combined, they create well-rounded individuals ready to lead in any arena of life.

Looking Ahead

Strong individuals make strong communities, but communities need intentional connection to thrive. In the next chapter, we will explore **Building & Sustaining Community Relationships**—the glue that holds all poverty-breaking strategies together.

Chapter 14 – Building & Sustaining Community Relationships

Why Relationships Are the Glue of Transformation

No leader, organization, or initiative can break the cycle of poverty alone. Real change happens when communities come together—sharing resources, aligning goals, and working toward a shared vision. Strong community relationships are the infrastructure that supports every program, policy, and opportunity. Without them, even the best-designed strategies can fail to take root.

The Foundation of Trust

Community relationships are built on trust, and trust is earned over time through consistency, transparency, and mutual respect. In communities affected by poverty, mistrust of institutions is often high due to a history of broken promises, short-term interventions, and outside agendas. Leaders must work intentionally to:

- Listen before acting.

- Show up consistently, not just during crises.
- Keep commitments and follow through on promises.
- Involve community members in decision-making, not just as recipients of services.

The Benefits of Strong Community Networks

When relationships are healthy and partnerships are strong, communities gain:

- **Resource Sharing** – Organizations can pool funding, staff, and expertise for greater impact.
- **Unified Advocacy** – A collective voice has more influence on policy and funding decisions.
- **Faster Problem-Solving** – Challenges are addressed more effectively when communication channels are open.
- **Long-Term Stability** – Trust-based partnerships weather changes in leadership, funding, and political climate.

Strategies for Building and Sustaining Relationships

1. **Collaborative Planning** – Include multiple stakeholders—residents, nonprofits, businesses, schools—in designing programs.

2. **Regular Communication** – Host community forums, newsletters, and open-door meetings to keep dialogue flowing.

3. **Shared Wins** – Celebrate successes publicly and give credit to all involved partners.

4. **Conflict Resolution** – Address tensions quickly and fairly to prevent breakdowns in trust.

5. **Long-Term Commitment** – Prioritize relationships over quick results, knowing real change takes years.

The Role of Leaders as Bridge Builders

Leaders are uniquely positioned to connect people and resources that might not otherwise meet. Whether it's introducing a local business owner to a youth program coordinator, or bringing city officials into conversation with grassroots advocates, leaders can catalyze connections that spark new opportunities.

Case Example: A Network That Outlasted the Grant

In one city, a coalition of schools, nonprofits, and small businesses came together around a youth employment initiative. When the initial funding ended, the network didn't dissolve—because the relationships had become stronger than the original project. They continued working together, attracting new resources, and expanding their efforts over the years.

Relationships as a Long-Term Asset

Community relationships are like social capital—they grow in value over time when invested in. They provide stability in times of uncertainty and accelerate progress when opportunities arise. For leaders committed to breaking poverty, these relationships are not optional—they are essential.

Looking Ahead

Community relationships give us strength, but they must be paired with active participation in shaping the systems that affect our lives. In the next chapter, we'll explore **The Power of Civic Engagement**—how mobilizing communities to participate in decision-making creates lasting, systemic change.

Chapter 15 – The Power of Civic Engagement

Why Civic Engagement Is Non-Negotiable

Building strong community relationships lays the groundwork for trust and collaboration. But to secure lasting change, communities must move from connection to *collective action*. Civic engagement—participation in the political, social, and policy-making processes—ensures that the voices of those most affected by poverty help shape the systems that govern them.

Without civic engagement, decisions are made for communities instead of with them. This can lead to policies that overlook real needs, waste resources, or even deepen inequality. When communities actively participate, they influence laws, budgets, and initiatives that directly impact their prosperity.

Beyond Voting

Voting is a critical part of civic engagement, but it's not the whole picture. Civic engagement includes:

- Attending public meetings and town halls.

- Serving on advisory boards, committees, and councils.

- Participating in public consultations on community projects.
- Organizing or joining advocacy campaigns.
- Building relationships with elected officials to communicate community priorities.

The Benefits of Active Participation

Communities that are civically engaged:

- Gain more equitable access to funding and resources.
- Influence the design of programs that serve them.
- Build accountability into local government and institutions.
- Develop a stronger sense of ownership and pride in their neighborhoods.

The Leader's Role in Civic Engagement

Leaders can cultivate civic engagement by:

- **Educating** community members on how local government works and how decisions are made.
- **Facilitating access** to meetings, hearings, and voting

through transportation, childcare, and translation services.

- **Mobilizing networks** to turn out for key decision-making moments.

- **Mentoring emerging leaders** to run for office or take public service roles.

Overcoming Barriers to Engagement

Barriers to civic participation—such as distrust of institutions, time constraints, or lack of information—must be addressed head-on. Leaders should acknowledge these realities and work to remove them through consistent outreach, clear communication, and visible results from participation.

Case Example: From Silence to Influence

In one city, a coalition of neighborhood leaders began organizing regular "community-to-council" sessions where residents could practice presenting their concerns before attending official meetings. Within a year, several community priorities were adopted into the city's strategic plan, including expanded job training and affordable housing initiatives.

Civic Engagement as a Path to Systemic Change

Civic engagement turns community energy into structural change. It ensures that progress made through programs, partnerships, and personal development is supported—rather than hindered—by laws, policies, and public investment.

Looking Ahead

Civic engagement builds influence, but to break poverty's grip at scale, we must pair influence with innovation. In the next chapter, we will explore **Scaling Impact Through Innovation**—how creative problem-solving and modern tools can multiply results and accelerate transformation.

Chapter 16 – Scaling Impact Through Innovation

Why Innovation Is Essential for Growth

Breaking the cycle of poverty requires more than repeating what has worked in the past—it demands reimagining what's possible. Even the most effective programs can only go so far if they aren't designed to adapt, expand, and serve more people over time. Innovation is the key to scaling impact without losing quality or focus.

Innovation doesn't always mean inventing something new; it often means applying fresh thinking, new tools, or creative models to solve persistent problems in smarter, faster, and more sustainable ways.

The Challenge of Scaling

Scaling impact is about multiplying results without multiplying costs at the same rate. Common challenges include:

- Limited funding for expansion.
- Difficulty maintaining quality as reach grows.
- Resistance to change from stakeholders used to "the

old way."

- Technology or infrastructure gaps that slow growth.

These obstacles are real, but they can be overcome with intentional planning and a willingness to innovate.

Types of Innovation That Drive Scale

1. **Process Innovation** – Streamlining systems to make programs more efficient and accessible.
2. **Technological Innovation** – Using digital tools, data analytics, and online platforms to reach more people.
3. **Partnership Innovation** – Leveraging unconventional alliances to expand reach and resources.
4. **Financial Innovation** – Developing sustainable funding models such as social enterprises, impact investing, or hybrid nonprofit/for-profit structures.
5. **Programmatic Innovation** – Adapting services to meet evolving community needs without losing core mission.

The Leader's Role in Driving Innovation

Leaders are the catalysts of change when they:

- Encourage a culture of experimentation—allowing for

smart risks and learning from failures.

- Actively seek input from those being served, ensuring solutions are user-centered.
- Stay informed on emerging trends and technologies.
- Share knowledge openly so others can replicate successful models.

Case Example: Technology-Enabled Expansion

A workforce development program that once trained 50 people per year in person shifted to a hybrid model with online learning modules and virtual mentorship. Within two years, it was serving 500 participants across multiple regions—without proportionally increasing staff or costs.

From Innovation to Transformation

When innovation is intentional, it doesn't just expand reach—it improves outcomes. It allows solutions to evolve with the community's needs and ensures that the impact is not limited to one location, time, or leadership team.

Looking Ahead

Innovation can scale change, but it must be paired with accountability to ensure results are real and lasting. In the next chapter, we will explore **Measuring Success and Adapting**—how to track progress, learn from challenges, and keep momentum over the long term.

Chapter 17 – Measuring Success and Adapting

Why Measurement Matters

In the fight against poverty, good intentions are not enough. If we cannot measure results, we cannot prove impact, secure support, or refine our strategies. Measurement transforms leadership from guesswork into informed decision-making. It ensures that the resources invested—time, money, and human energy—are producing real change.

Leaders who measure success consistently are able to celebrate wins, identify gaps, and adapt to shifting conditions. This agility is what turns short-term initiatives into long-term, sustainable solutions.

Defining What Success Looks Like

Every initiative should begin with a clear vision of success. That might include:

- **Quantitative Metrics** – Number of people trained, jobs created, or businesses launched.
- **Qualitative Metrics** – Testimonials, improved confidence, or changes in community culture.

- **Systemic Metrics** – Policy changes, reduced unemployment rates, or improved health outcomes.

Defining success up front ensures everyone—leaders, partners, funders, and community members—works toward the same goals.

Tools and Methods for Measuring Impact

1. **Surveys and Feedback Loops** – Direct input from participants to gauge satisfaction and relevance.
2. **Data Tracking Systems** – Software to monitor progress against key performance indicators (KPIs).
3. **Case Studies** – Documenting detailed stories that illustrate the real-world effects of programs.
4. **Benchmarking** – Comparing results to similar programs or community averages.
5. **Longitudinal Tracking** – Following participants over time to measure sustained change.

The Role of Adaptation in Sustaining Impact

Measurement is not just about proving what works—it's about discovering what doesn't, and making adjustments. Leaders committed to breaking the cycle of poverty must:

- Be open to changing strategies based on evidence.

- Pilot new approaches before scaling them.
- Involve stakeholders in decision-making about program changes.
- Celebrate progress while remaining honest about areas for improvement.

Case Example: Course-Correcting for Greater Results

A youth development program noticed through tracking that participants were excelling academically but struggling to find jobs after graduation. Instead of accepting partial success, the leadership team added workforce training and employer partnerships. Within a year, job placement rates tripled—demonstrating the power of adapting based on real data.

Closing the Loop

When leaders measure success and adapt accordingly, they create a continuous cycle of improvement. This not only builds credibility with funders and partners but also keeps momentum alive, ensuring that efforts remain relevant and effective in changing conditions.

DTD'S LEADERSHIP PLAYBOOK & BLUEPRINT

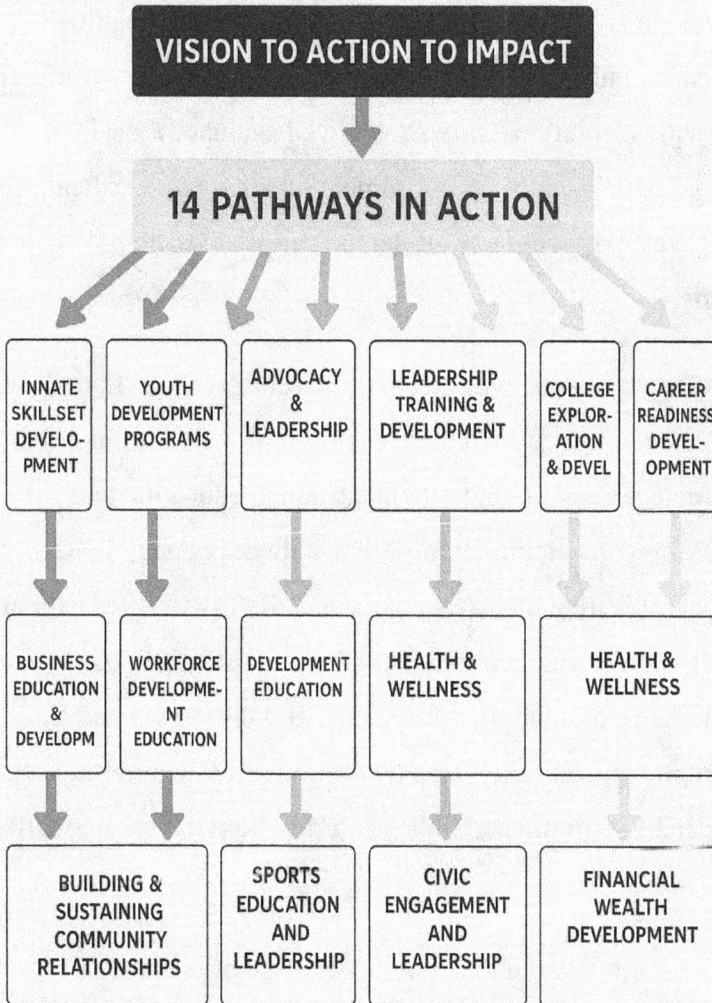

VISION TO ACTION TO IMPACT

14 PATHWAYS IN ACTION

INNATE SKILLSET DEVELO-PMENT	YOUTH DEVELOPMENT PROGRAMS	ADVOCACY & LEADERSHIP	LEADERSHIP TRAINING & DEVELOPMENT	COLLEGE EXPLOR-ATION & DEVEL	CAREER READINESS DEVEL-OPMENT

BUSINESS EDUCATION & DEVELOPM	WORKFORCE DEVELOPME-NT EDUCATION	DEVELOPMENT EDUCATION	HEALTH & WELLNESS	HEALTH & WELLNESS

BUILDING & SUSTAINING COMMUNITY RELATIONSHIPS	SPORTS EDUCATION AND LEADERSHIP	CIVIC ENGAGEMENT AND LEADERSHIP	FINANCIAL WEALTH DEVELOPMENT

Global Transition into Prologue

The fourteen pathways outlined in my earlier works demonstrated how poverty can be disrupted through skill development, education, family empowerment, health, business, and community engagement. Each pathway offered a practical solution, yet when viewed against the scale of global poverty, they reveal something even more critical: **no single effort, program, or sector can dismantle poverty alone.**

Across continents, we see this truth reinforced. In Latin America, targeted cash transfer programs lifted millions from extreme poverty—yet without sustained education and workforce development, progress stalled. In Asia, rapid industrialization created unprecedented growth—yet without health equity and community infrastructure, millions remained excluded. In Africa, microfinance empowered entrepreneurs at the village level—yet without systemic leadership training and policy reform, those gains often failed to scale.

These lessons remind us that poverty is not just a local condition; it is a **global challenge demanding integrated solutions**. Leaders today must think beyond silos, beyond borders, and beyond short-term relief. They must adopt frameworks that connect vision to measurable outcomes, and individual pathways to systemic transformation.

That is why this book advances the *Vision* → *Action* → *Impact* model. It is more than theory—it is a leadership roadmap tested by diverse global examples and designed to equip both established and aspiring leaders to move beyond managing poverty and begin **breaking it, sustainably and at scale**.

The *Prologue* that follows sets this stage: explaining why poverty, though persistent, is not permanent—and why leaders across every sector, in every nation, must see themselves as part of the solution.

Prologue – The Leadership Imperative to End Poverty

From Witness to Warrior: Why I Lead This Work

I did not arrive at this mission by chance. Like many leaders driven to change the world, my calling is the result of both lived experience and intentional observation. Poverty is not an abstract figure in a report to me—it is a reality I have stood inside.

I have seen its weight in the restless eyes of parents calculating which bill they can afford to pay this month. I have walked through schools where ceilings leak and supplies run out long before the end of term, yet the children inside possess minds capable of solving global crises—if only given the chance. I have met leaders in villages, cities, and boardrooms who long to solve the problem but feel dwarfed by its complexity.

And yet, I have seen the other side.
I have seen the spark of confidence in a young person discovering their talent. I have seen communities rise when given access to opportunity. I have seen women form

cooperatives to educate their children, and entrepreneurs in remote regions build sustainable businesses from microloans.

These experiences have convinced me of one unwavering truth: **poverty is not permanent**. It may be deep-rooted, but it can be broken—when leaders choose to lead with vision, courage, and persistence.

The True Cost of Accepting Poverty

The greatest danger in our time is not that poverty exists, but that too many have quietly accepted it as inevitable. This acceptance carries a price no nation can afford:

- Innovation slows when billions of minds are locked out of solving the world's challenges.
- Relief efforts replace transformation, creating dependency rather than independence.
- Structural inequities remain unchallenged, passing disadvantage from one generation to the next.

Globally, over 700 million people live in extreme poverty. Progress, while real, has slowed—and in some regions reversed. Climate change, conflict, and inequality threaten to undo decades of gains. This is not just a humanitarian crisis; it is a **leadership crisis**—one that demands new thinking, new coalitions, and a refusal to settle for "managing" the problem.

From Management to Mastery: Breaking the Cycle

Too often, our strategies aim to **manage poverty**, not eliminate it. We provide food without building food systems. We give temporary housing without solving housing access. We create jobs without ensuring career growth.

These interventions are critical—but they are not the endgame. Managing poverty is like patching a leaking roof while the foundation rots. It is a relief without renewal.

To truly break the cycle, leaders must:

- Equip people with skills and education that lead to mobility.
- Ensure access to capital and markets for entrepreneurs.
- Shift the narrative so that people are seen as partners in their own progress, not passive recipients of charity.

This is **capacity building**—an investment in human potential that multiplies returns for families, communities, and economies.

The Global Leadership Gap

The poverty crisis is not a shortage of goodwill; it is a shortage of **aligned, prepared, and collaborative leadership**. Many work tirelessly in isolation—governments here, nonprofits there, businesses elsewhere—but without integration, efforts remain fragmented.

Leaders capable of dismantling poverty:

- Understand both the visible symptoms and the hidden systems that keep poverty in place.
- Dare to disrupt the status quo when it no longer serves.
- Unite stakeholders from vastly different sectors toward shared, measurable goals.
- Judge success not by how many are helped, but by how many no longer need help.

The proof is already in motion: Rwanda's coordinated governance and private-sector investment, Bangladesh's microcredit revolution, Medellín's transformation from violence to opportunity. In each case, **prepared leaders** moved beyond relief toward systemic change.

The Vision → Action → Impact Model

This book offers a universal framework for leaders everywhere: **Vision → Action → Impact**.

- **Vision – See Beyond the Present.** Leaders must envision a future where poverty is not the dominant story. This vision must be specific enough to inspire and bold enough to rally action. Weak vision yields weak results. Strong vision attracts resources and unites people.
- **Action – Move from Idea to Implementation.** Strategy without execution is wishful thinking. Action means measurable steps—policy reforms, partnerships, investments—that dismantle the barriers to upward mobility.
- **Impact – Deliver and Sustain Results.** Impact is not a one-year improvement; it is generational change. It means healthier communities, stronger families, and children inheriting opportunity instead of disadvantage.

This model is adaptable, scalable, and sustainable. It works in rural and urban settings, in developed and developing nations alike. And it works because it is not about a single leader doing it all—it is about **creating the conditions for many leaders to rise**.

A Global Call to Lead

Poverty is complex, but complexity does not equal impossibility. We have the examples, the research, and the proof that cycles can be broken. What remains is the willingness to lead differently—bolder, faster, together.

This book is written for leaders and aspiring leaders in every corner of the globe. It is for executives and educators, policymakers and grassroots organizers, entrepreneurs and faith leaders. Wherever you are, you have influence. Wherever you lead, you can apply Vision → Action → Impact.

Read with your mind open and your heart engaged. See your role not as a spectator but as an architect of solutions. The clock is ticking—and the world needs leaders who will not only imagine a poverty-free future but take decisive action to build it.

WHY POVERTY CAN BE BROKEN

GLOBAL POVERTY IN NUMBERS

700+ million
people live in extreme poverty worldwide

9%
of the alobal population ives on less than $215 • day

575 million
people projected to still live in extreme poverty in 2090

LEADING STRATEGIES FOR BREAKING THE CYCLE

SKILL-BUILDING
Empowering people through education and training

ACCESS TO RESOURCES
Providing capital, opportunities, and support

NARRATIVE TRANSFORMATION
Reframing mindsets to see potential and possibility

KEY LEADERSHIP TRAITS

- Understanding structural causes of poverty

- Innovating to challenge the status quo

- Building diverse coalitions for change

- Foousing on outcomes rather than outputs

THE VISION → ACTION → IMPACT FRAMEWOR

VISION
Envisioning a future where poverty is not inevitable

ACTION
Turning vision into tangible programs and initiatives

IMPACT
Measuring sustainable, long-term improvements

Part I – The Leadership Foundation

Chapter 1 – Harnessing Innate Potential: The Leader's Role in Unlocking Human Capital

The Untapped Wealth in People

The most valuable resource on earth is not oil, rare minerals, or technology—it's human potential.

Yet, in too many communities, especially those experiencing persistent poverty, this resource is left dormant.

According to the **World Economic Forum, more than 40% of the world's human capital is underutilized**—meaning billions of people's skills, creativity, and leadership capacity go untapped. In low-income areas, the percentage is even higher, creating an unnecessary loss of innovation, productivity, and economic growth.

Poverty is not simply a lack of money; it is the systematic neglect of talent. It is the loss of ideas that could have launched businesses, healed communities, or solved global problems—if only they had been nurtured.

Innate Skills: The Hidden Power in Every Person

Every human being is born with innate skills—problem-solving ability, adaptability, creativity, leadership instincts. These abilities are not confined to people with elite degrees or privileged backgrounds; they are universal.

The challenge is that **poverty often hides these abilities behind daily survival struggles**. Leaders, whether in business, government, or nonprofit sectors, must see past the surface to discover the latent strengths in people.

Example: Barefoot College, India

This initiative trains rural women—most of whom are illiterate—to become solar engineers, water technicians, and educators. These women, often grandmothers, go on to electrify entire villages and train others. Their success demonstrates that the capacity to innovate is not the exclusive domain of the formally educated—it's a human trait waiting to be activated.

What Are Innate Skills?

Innate skills are natural talents, tendencies, or aptitudes that someone possesses without formal training. They might be:

- A knack for **problem-solving** under pressure.
- The ability to **connect with people** and build trust.
- Creativity in **art, design, or innovation**.
- Strong **mechanical or technical instincts**, such as fixing equipment or working with tools.
- Leadership potential shown in community or peer group settings.

These skills often go unnoticed or undervalued because the individual is too focused on surviving day-to-day challenges to recognize them as assets.

Why Leaders Must Focus on Skill Discovery

In communities impacted by poverty, there is often no structured process for identifying and cultivating talent. Traditional systems—schools, hiring processes, and even some training programs—tend to focus on deficits rather than strengths. Leaders can reverse this by making skill discovery a central part of any development initiative.

Practical ways to do this include:

- **Skill Mapping** – Hosting workshops where participants list hobbies, past jobs, and personal interests to uncover hidden skills.

- **Observation** – Watching how individuals approach challenges and identifying natural problem-solvers, communicators, or organizers.

- **Peer Feedback** – Encouraging group members to point out strengths they've seen in each other.

The Skill Development Cycle

Developing innate skills into tools for prosperity involves three phases:

1. **Discovery** – Helping individuals recognize what they already do well.
2. **Development** – Providing training and resources to refine these skills into market-ready competencies.
3. **Deployment** – Connecting individuals with opportunities to apply their skills in paid work, entrepreneurship, or leadership roles.

This cycle is continuous—each new opportunity can lead to new skills, which in turn create more opportunities.

Bridging the Gap Between Talent and Opportunity

One of the greatest frustrations for people with untapped talent is not knowing how to translate it into income or advancement. Leaders must build bridges between raw ability and real-world opportunity.

Examples include:

- Connecting a skilled home cook with culinary training and a pathway to restaurant ownership.
- Guiding a mechanically inclined youth into an apprenticeship with a local tradesperson.
- Pairing a natural communicator with training in sales, customer service, or public relations.

This bridge-building often requires partnerships with businesses, trade schools, nonprofits, and community organizations that can offer specialized training and job placement.

The Role of Soft Skills

While technical skills are essential, **soft skills**—such as communication, adaptability, time management, and teamwork—are equally important in breaking poverty cycles.

Many people lose opportunities not because they lack technical knowledge, but because they struggle with workplace expectations.

Leaders should incorporate soft skills training into all development programs, ensuring that participants can thrive in both professional and entrepreneurial settings.

Removing Barriers to Skill Development

Even when individuals are motivated and capable, barriers like transportation, childcare, financial constraints, and scheduling conflicts can derail skill development. Leaders must proactively address these barriers by:

- Offering flexible training schedules.
- Providing stipends or childcare support.
- Hosting programs in accessible community spaces.
- Partnering with employers to cover training costs in exchange for future employment.

A Story of Transformation

I once worked with a woman named Marissa who had been a stay-at-home mother for over a decade. She believed she had "no real skills" to offer an employer. Through a skill-mapping exercise, we discovered her strengths in organization, budgeting, and event planning—skills she had honed managing her household and community events. With targeted training in project management software and small business operations, she transitioned into a full-time role coordinating events for a local nonprofit. Within two years, she started her own event-planning business.

Her skills had always been there; they just needed to be recognized, developed, and applied.

Why Innate Skillset Development Is a Poverty Breaker

When people learn to leverage what they already have, they no longer see themselves as limited by what they lack. Skill development shifts identity—from "someone who needs help" to "someone who adds value." This shift in self-perception is as important as the skills themselves, because it fuels confidence, initiative, and long-term growth.

Looking Ahead

With new mindsets and marketable skills in place, we can focus on where the change begins for the next generation. In the next chapter, we'll explore **Youth Development as the**

Cornerstone—how investing early creates exponential returns for individuals, families, and communities.

Why Leaders Must Champion Skill Discovery

Leaders and aspiring leaders have the ability—and the responsibility—to create systems that uncover and develop innate skills. This is not just a humanitarian effort; it is a strategic economic decision.

When leaders invest in human capital, they:

- Expand the skilled labor force.
- Strengthen community resilience against economic shocks.
- Build trust and engagement between people and institutions.

A workforce that is both skilled and self-confident can transform local economies from the inside out.

From Discovery to Development

Identifying potential is only step one. Development requires:

1. **Access to Training** – Affordable, relevant, and culturally responsive programs.
2. **Mentorship** – Guidance from experienced leaders who can help avoid common pitfalls.
3. **Real-World Application** – Opportunities for people to apply what they learn in environments that challenge and stretch their capabilities.

Case Study: Rwanda's Digital Ambassadors Program

In Rwanda, young leaders are trained to teach digital literacy in rural areas. Many of these trainers had no formal tech background themselves but were quick learners with natural teaching skills. The program has brought thousands of citizens online, opening economic and educational opportunities previously out of reach.

The Leadership Mindset Shift

Too many organizations treat people as fixed assets—capable only of what their current résumé says. Leaders committed to breaking poverty must adopt a different mindset: **people are expandable assets** whose capacity grows with investment.

This means:

- Recruiting for potential, not just credentials.
- Designing promotions and leadership tracks for those traditionally overlooked.
- Measuring success by how many people grow under your leadership, not just by your own achievements.

Global Leadership Insights

- **Africa**: Youth skill development programs, like those in Ghana's coding bootcamps, are producing tech entrepreneurs without formal degrees.
- **Latin America**: Cooperative farming initiatives in Colombia are turning subsistence farmers into agribusiness leaders.
- **Asia**: Community-led micro-manufacturing projects in Vietnam have empowered women to lead export-based enterprises.

These examples prove that when leaders create **structures for capacity building**, innate skills evolve into marketable, community-strengthening abilities.

Call to Action for Leaders

- **Audit Your Circle**: Who around you has untapped skills?

- **Create Skill Discovery Platforms**: This could be as simple as community workshops or as complex as company-wide innovation challenges.
- **Mentor and Multiply**: For every person you train, challenge them to train another—doubling the leadership pipeline.

Breaking poverty begins when leaders make a non-negotiable commitment to see, invest in, and unleash the potential that already exists.

Chapter 2 – Youth Empowerment as a Global Economic Strategy

The Untapped Engine of Growth

The world's youth population—those aged 15 to 24—stands at **1.2 billion**, the largest in history. Nearly **90% live in developing countries**, where economic opportunities are often scarce (**UNFPA**). This demographic reality presents both a monumental opportunity and a monumental risk:

- **Opportunity**: An educated, engaged, and empowered youth population can fuel innovation, productivity, and sustainable growth for decades.
- **Risk**: If undereducated, underemployed, and excluded from leadership, this same generation can deepen cycles of poverty and social instability.

According to the **International Labour Organization**, youth unemployment rates arc consistently two to three times higher than those of adults. For millions, this means years of economic stagnation just as they are entering the workforce.

Why Youth Development is an Economic Imperative

Investing in young people is not a charitable act—it is an **economic growth strategy**. The **OECD** notes that a 10% increase in secondary school completion rates among youth correlates with an annual GDP growth increase of 0.3% in developing countries.

Youth empowerment affects:

- **Innovation capacity** – Young people bring fresh ideas and are more likely to adopt and adapt to new technologies.
- **Demographic dividends** – When youth enter the workforce with strong skills, they can outpace dependency rates, fueling economic expansion.
- **Social stability** – Empowered youth are less vulnerable to crime, extremism, and displacement.

From Passive Recipients to Active Leaders

Too often, youth development programs frame young people as passive recipients of help. True empowerment flips the script, positioning them as **partners and decision-makers** in shaping their futures.

Case Study: Rwanda's YouthConnekt

Launched in 2012, YouthConnekt connects young Rwandans with mentorship, entrepreneurship training, and digital skills development. Over 13 million youth have been reached, and the program has created thousands of jobs. Its success lies in giving youth **ownership of their growth**, with government and private sector leaders acting as enablers, not controllers.

The Role of Leadership in Youth Empowerment

Leaders who want to break cycles of poverty through youth empowerment must:

1. **Champion Education Reform** – Ensure curricula include critical thinking, technology skills, and entrepreneurship.
2. **Create Entry Points to Leadership** – Invite young voices into decision-making spaces.
3. **Build Mentorship Ecosystems** – Link youth to role models across industries.

Global Examples of Youth-Driven Transformation

- **Africa**: Kenya's Ajira Digital Program trains young people in online freelance skills, connecting them to the global gig economy.
- **Asia**: India's Skill India mission aims to train over 400 million people in market-relevant skills by 2025.
- **Latin America**: Colombia's Jóvenes en Acción offers cash transfers conditional on skills training participation, incentivizing both education and workforce readiness.

These examples show that **when leaders invest in the capacity and leadership of youth, they invest in the economic future of their nations**.

Leadership Mindset Shift

The most effective leaders see youth not as "the leaders of tomorrow" but as **leaders of today**. They recognize that giving young people responsibility and resources now creates a multiplier effect—each empowered young leader influences peers, family members, and future generations.

Call to Action for Leaders

- Identify the top three barriers facing young people in your community—are they skills-based, access-based, or systemic?
- Partner with educational institutions, businesses, and nonprofits to co-design solutions.
- Create measurable goals for youth involvement in leadership and track progress annually.

The future is not something we prepare youth for—it is something we build with them.

Chapter 3 – Leadership as Advocacy: Influencing Systems for Lasting Change

Why Advocacy is Non-Negotiable for Leaders Fighting Poverty

Poverty doesn't happen in a vacuum—it is sustained, and sometimes deepened, by **systems**: policies, regulations, and institutional practices that shape access to resources, education, housing, and economic opportunity.

According to the **Brookings Institution**, more than **half of the poverty reduction in OECD countries over the past 30 years** can be attributed to policy changes—not just market forces. That means leadership in poverty reduction is not just about running programs or funding initiatives—it's about **changing the rules of the game**.

From Charity to Systemic Change

Direct service—providing food, shelter, or temporary work—changes lives in the moment.

Advocacy changes lives for generations.

The difference is scope:

- **Direct service** solves immediate needs.
- **Advocacy** solves the root causes of those needs.

Without advocacy, the systems that produce poverty remain in place, forcing communities to fight the same battles over and over again.

Case Study: Brazil's Bolsa Família Program

Launched in 2003, Bolsa Família provided conditional cash transfers to low-income families, requiring school attendance and regular health checkups for children. Initially modest, it grew into one of the largest poverty reduction programs in the world.

Its success was not an accident—it was the result of **sustained advocacy** from civil society, economists, and community leaders who pushed the government to scale the program. Within a decade, extreme poverty in Brazil dropped from 9.7% to 4.3%, and school attendance rates in targeted communities surged.

The Leadership Skills Behind Effective Advocacy

1. **Data Mastery** – Leaders must be fluent in the numbers that drive policy discussions: poverty rates, economic multipliers, cost-benefit analyses.
2. **Coalition Building** – Advocacy requires aligning businesses, nonprofits, government agencies, and the communities most affected.
3. **Strategic Persistence** – System change often takes years. Leaders must be prepared for long-term engagement beyond political cycles.

Global Examples of Advocacy in Action

- **Kenya**: Advocacy campaigns led to the introduction of free primary education in 2003, enrolling 1.5 million more children within the first year.
- **United States**: The Earned Income Tax Credit, expanded through bipartisan advocacy, has lifted millions of families above the poverty line.
- **Philippines**: Grassroots campaigns against exploitative lending resulted in microfinance regulations that protect low-income borrowers.

The Role of Business Leaders in Advocacy

Some leaders hesitate to engage in policy debates, fearing political controversy. But **business leaders** are uniquely positioned to influence systems because:

- They understand the workforce impact of poverty.
- They can mobilize resources quickly.
- They have credibility with policymakers on economic issues.

By leveraging their influence, business leaders can advocate for workforce training incentives, affordable housing development, and equitable lending practices.

Call to Action for Leaders

- Identify one systemic barrier in your community that, if removed, would significantly reduce poverty.
- Map the stakeholders who have the power to change it.
- Commit to building or joining a coalition to address it within the next 12 months.

Leadership that does not engage in advocacy risks becoming a caretaker of poverty, rather than a

dismantler of it.

Chapter 4 – Transformative Leadership Training: Equipping Leaders to Dismantle Poverty

Why Leadership Development is a Poverty Reduction Strategy

Poverty persists in part because **there aren't enough trained, visionary leaders** equipped to challenge the systems that sustain it.
 While passion for change is essential, passion without skill can lead to fragmented efforts, wasted resources, and stalled progress.

According to the **World Bank**, countries and communities with strong, transparent, and inclusive leadership systems see up to **3% higher annual GDP growth** than those with weaker leadership pipelines. Leadership capability is directly tied to economic stability, institutional trust, and social mobility.

From Positional Power to Transformational Influence

Transformative leadership is not about holding titles—it's about **mobilizing people and resources to create systemic change**. The leaders who dismantle poverty:

- Inspire vision and trust.
- Build multi-sector coalitions.
- Use evidence-based strategies, not guesswork.
- Develop other leaders, ensuring change outlasts their tenure.

Case Study: Singapore's Leadership Pipeline

Singapore invests heavily in leadership development across both public and private sectors. Leaders are rotated through diverse roles, exposed to international perspectives, and trained in crisis management. This strategic investment transformed Singapore from a low-income nation in the 1960s into one of the most competitive economies in the world today.

The Leadership Gap in Poverty Solutions

Even in countries with vibrant economies, leadership gaps exist in communities where poverty is entrenched. These gaps are not just about **how many** leaders there are—they're about **how prepared** those leaders are to address complex, interconnected challenges.

Leadership development in poverty-focused work often suffers from:

- **Short-term focus**: Workshops with no follow-up.
- **Siloed learning**: Leaders trained in isolation from other sectors.
- **Underinvestment**: Minimal resources allocated to leadership training.

Core Competencies for Poverty-Focused Leadership

1. **Systems Thinking** – Understanding how education, health, housing, and economics interact.
2. **Advocacy Skills** – Navigating political landscapes to influence policy.
3. **Financial Acumen** – Managing budgets, investments, and funding streams.
4. **Cultural Intelligence** – Leading effectively across diverse communities.

Global Examples of Leadership Training Impact

- **Rwanda**: The *Imbuto Foundation* develops young leaders with mentorship and scholarship programs, producing a generation ready to lead national development.
- **Brazil**: The *Lemann Foundation* offers advanced training for educators and community leaders, directly improving education outcomes in low-income areas.
- **Kenya**: *Akili Dada* trains young women leaders, many of whom now lead organizations and influence policy.

Building a Scalable Leadership Development Model

Leaders and institutions must commit to:

- **Embedding Leadership in Education** – Leadership skills should be taught alongside literacy and numeracy in schools.
- **Cross-Sector Fellowships** – Place emerging leaders in business, government, and nonprofit roles to build versatility.
- **Continuous Learning** – Leadership development must be ongoing, not one-and-done.

Call to Action for Leaders

- Audit your organization's leadership pipeline: Are you producing problem-solvers or problem-managers?
- Commit resources—time, budget, mentorship—to leadership training.
- Measure success not by the number of leaders trained, but by the **systems they improve and the lives they impact**.

To break the cycle of poverty, we must break the habit of leaving leadership development to chance.

Part II – Education and Opportunity

Chapter 5 – Expanding Horizons: College Exploration as a Pathway to Prosperity

Why Higher Education Access Matters in the Fight Against Poverty

Education remains one of the most powerful drivers of social mobility. According to the **World Bank**, each additional year of schooling can increase an individual's earnings by an average of **10%**, and higher education degrees can lead to earnings up to **three times greater** than those without.

But for many in low-income communities, higher education isn't a realistic option—it's a distant concept, obscured by financial barriers, limited guidance, and a lack of visible role models. College exploration is not just about academics; it's about **exposing individuals to possibilities they may never have imagined**.

The Access Gap

Barriers to higher education often include:

- **Financial constraints**: Tuition, living costs, and hidden fees.
- **Information gaps**: Lack of guidance on application processes, scholarships, and career alignment.
- **Cultural barriers**: Low college attendance norms in certain communities.

The **UNESCO Global Education Monitoring Report** notes that only **9% of young people in low-income countries** attend higher education institutions, compared to 77% in high-income countries. This disparity perpetuates cycles of economic inequality on a global scale.

From Awareness to Aspiration

College exploration programs that break poverty cycles do more than present information—they **ignite aspiration**. They connect students with mentors, expose them to diverse fields of study, and link education to real-world economic opportunities.

Case Study: The Posse Foundation, USA

By recruiting cohorts ("posses") of high-potential students from underrepresented backgrounds and placing them in supportive peer groups at top universities, the Posse

Foundation boasts a **90% graduation rate**—far above the U.S. national average. The program's success lies in blending access with mentorship and leadership development.

The Leadership Role in Expanding Access

Leaders who champion higher education as a poverty reduction tool must:

1. **Invest in Early Exposure** – College readiness starts long before the application process.
2. **Build Bridges Between Schools and Universities** – Establish partnerships for dual-enrollment programs, campus visits, and mentorship.
3. **Advocate for Financial Support** – Push for scholarship programs, tuition assistance, and policies that reduce student debt.

Global Examples of Higher Education Access Efforts

- **Brazil**: The University for All Program (ProUni) offers scholarships to low-income students at private universities, greatly expanding access for disadvantaged youth.

- **South Africa**: The National Student Financial Aid Scheme provides means-tested loans and bursaries, resulting in higher enrollment from low-income communities.
- **Bangladesh**: BRAC University integrates financial support with leadership training, producing graduates who return to serve in rural development roles.

Aligning Higher Education with Economic Opportunity

For higher education to be an effective poverty reduction tool, it must be **aligned with market needs**. Degrees that do not connect to employable skills risk saddling students with debt without improving their economic future. Leaders must encourage institutions to:

- Integrate entrepreneurship into curricula.
- Partner with industries for internships and job placement.
- Continuously update programs based on labor market trends.

Call to Action for Leaders

- Sponsor college visits and information sessions for students in low-income areas.
- Create scholarship funds targeted at first-generation college students.

- Establish mentorship networks that guide students from application through graduation and into careers.

Higher education access is not just a personal achievement—it is a community investment with generational returns.

Chapter 6 – Career Readiness Development: Building Pathways to Sustainable Employment

Why Career Readiness Is More Than Job Training

Getting a job is not the same as building a sustainable career. While entry-level employment can provide immediate income, without the skills, networks, and growth opportunities to advance, many individuals remain trapped in **low-wage, high-turnover positions**—unable to break free from poverty.

The **International Labour Organization (ILO)** reports that **over 2 billion people worldwide work in informal or insecure jobs,** lacking protections, benefits, and upward mobility. Career readiness addresses this gap by preparing individuals for long-term employment that leads to economic stability and upward movement.

From Short-Term Employment to Long-Term Growth

Career readiness programs go beyond basic training to include:

- **Professional skills** – Communication, problem-solving, teamwork, and leadership.
- **Technical competencies** – Industry-specific knowledge that aligns with market demand.
- **Career navigation** – Understanding how to pursue promotions, negotiate salaries, and shift into leadership roles.

Case Study: Germany's Dual Education System

Germany integrates classroom learning with paid apprenticeships in industries like manufacturing, healthcare, and IT. This model has kept youth unemployment rates among the lowest in the world and produces graduates with both theoretical knowledge and hands-on experience.

Barriers to Career Readiness in Low-Income Communities

1. **Limited exposure** to high-growth industries.
2. **Lack of role models** in professional careers.

3. **Weak industry-school linkages** that leave training disconnected from employer needs.

According to the **World Economic Forum**, by 2030, **85 million jobs** may go unfilled globally due to skill gaps—while millions remain unemployed. Leaders have the power to close this gap through intentional partnerships and targeted skill-building initiatives.

The Leadership Role in Career Readiness

Leaders committed to breaking the poverty cycle through career readiness must:

1. **Align Programs with Market Demand** – Training must be relevant to sectors with job growth potential.
2. **Invest in Work-Based Learning** – Internships, apprenticeships, and job shadowing.
3. **Promote Lifelong Learning** – Encourage continual upskilling to remain competitive.

Global Examples of Career Readiness Initiatives

- **Singapore**: SkillsFuture credits empower citizens to continuously upgrade their skills throughout their careers.

- **Kenya**: Ajira Digital equips youth with skills for the global digital economy, creating freelancers who work with international clients.
- **United States**: Year Up provides urban young adults with technical and professional skills, along with corporate internships that lead to full-time employment.

Measuring Success in Career Readiness

Impact must be measured not just by job placement rates, but by:

- **Retention** – Are participants staying employed for more than two years?
- **Advancement** – Are they moving into higher-paying, higher-responsibility roles?
- **Income Growth** – Are wages increasing faster than inflation?

Call to Action for Leaders

- Partner with employers to co-design training programs that lead directly to job offers.

- Establish mentorship networks to guide workers through career transitions.
- Advocate for policies that support apprenticeships, workforce retraining, and wage growth.

Career readiness is the bridge between education and sustainable livelihoods. Without it, the promise of opportunity remains unfulfilled.

Chapter 7 – Business Education as a Tool for Inclusive Economic Growth

Why Business Education Matters in Poverty Reduction

While employment can provide stability, **entrepreneurship can create transformation**—not only for the individual but for the wider community. Business education equips people to generate their own income streams, create jobs for others, and build wealth that can be passed down to future generations.

The **Global Entrepreneurship Monitor (GEM)** notes that in low-income countries, small and medium enterprises (SMEs) account for **over 70% of employment**. Yet many entrepreneurs fail to scale because they lack **foundational business skills** such as financial management, marketing, and strategic planning.

From Hustle to Sustainable Enterprise

In many low-income communities, entrepreneurship begins out of necessity rather than opportunity. People start small ventures—selling food, crafts, or services—to survive. Without business education, these "survival businesses" often remain informal, vulnerable, and unable to grow.

Business education transforms these ventures into sustainable enterprises by teaching:

- **Financial literacy** – Understanding budgets, cash flow, and profit margins.
- **Market analysis** – Identifying and responding to customer needs.
- **Growth strategies** – Scaling operations, diversifying products, and entering new markets.

Case Study: Goldman Sachs 10,000 Women Initiative

Operating in more than 50 countries, this program provides women entrepreneurs with business and management education, mentoring, and networking. Alumni have reported **increased revenues and job creation**, directly impacting local economies and reducing poverty.

Barriers to Business Education Access

1. **Cost** – Training programs and courses are often

unaffordable for those who need them most.

2. **Location** – Programs may be concentrated in urban centers, inaccessible to rural entrepreneurs.

3. **Relevance** – Generic training that does not address local markets fails to create impact.

The Leadership Role in Expanding Business Education

Leaders can ensure business education becomes a **core pillar of poverty reduction strategies** by:

1. **Integrating Entrepreneurship into School Curricula** – Building skills early.

2. **Partnering with Private Sector Experts** – Offering mentorship and real-world perspectives.

3. **Supporting Localized Training Models** – Tailoring education to cultural and economic contexts.

Global Examples of Business Education Impact

- **Kenya**: The Equity Group Foundation's entrepreneurship program trains small business owners, resulting in higher survival rates and expansion into new markets.

- **Peru**: Technoserve's "Impulso" program helps farmers move from subsistence to export-level agribusiness.
- **Philippines**: Go Negosyo provides nationwide mentoring and capacity-building for micro-entrepreneurs, with government and corporate backing.

Aligning Business Education with Inclusive Growth

Business education is most effective when it's connected to broader economic systems:

- **Access to finance** – Linking graduates to microloans, grants, or investors.
- **Market linkages** – Helping entrepreneurs access supply chains and export opportunities.

- **Policy advocacy** – Reducing barriers to starting and scaling businesses.

Call to Action for Leaders

- Sponsor entrepreneurship workshops targeting underrepresented groups.
- Provide seed funding tied to completion of business education programs.
- Champion policies that create a business-friendly environment for small enterprises.

Business education doesn't just create entrepreneurs—it creates employers, innovators, and community builders.

Chapter 8 – Workforce Development Education: Aligning Skills with the Global Economy

Why Workforce Development Is Central to Breaking Poverty

Poverty reduction is not just about creating jobs—it's about creating **good jobs** and equipping people with the skills to fill them.

In today's rapidly evolving economy, industries are transforming faster than traditional education systems can keep up. Without deliberate workforce development strategies, millions will be left behind in low-wage, unstable employment.

The **World Economic Forum's Future of Jobs Report** predicts that by 2030, **more than one billion people worldwide will need to reskill** to meet changing labor demands. Failure to act risks widening the inequality gap and locking vulnerable populations out of growth industries.

From Skills Training to Workforce Systems

Workforce development is more than training individuals—it's about **building systems** that continuously adapt to industry trends and economic shifts. Effective workforce development:

- Aligns with **current and emerging labor market needs**.
- Integrates **education, employers, and policymakers** into a unified strategy.
- Provides **lifelong learning pathways** for career advancement.

Case Study: Switzerland's Vocational Education and Training (VET) Model

Over 70% of Swiss students participate in vocational programs that combine classroom learning with paid apprenticeships. This model ensures a near-seamless transition from education to the workforce and maintains one of the world's lowest youth unemployment rates.

Challenges in Workforce Development for Low-Income Communities

1. **Mismatch of Skills and Jobs** – Training in fields with low hiring demand.
2. **Limited Employer Engagement** – Companies not involved in shaping training programs.
3. **Barrier to Access** – Rural and underserved communities lacking infrastructure and resources for training.

According to the **OECD**, countries that maintain active employer partnerships in workforce programs experience **20% higher job placement rates**.

The Leadership Role in Workforce Development

Leaders in business, government, and education must work together to:

1. **Forecast Industry Needs** – Use labor market data to anticipate high-growth sectors.
2. **Design Responsive Programs** – Adapt curricula quickly to evolving technologies and demands.

3. **Remove Barriers** – Provide childcare, transportation, and financial assistance so training is accessible to all.

Global Examples of Workforce Development Excellence

- **Singapore**: SkillsFuture credits give every citizen funds for accredited training, encouraging lifelong upskilling.
- **Rwanda**: The Workforce Development Authority aligns training programs with national growth priorities such as tourism, manufacturing, and IT.
- **United States**: The Workforce Innovation and Opportunity Act (WIOA) supports regional partnerships to connect workers with in-demand industries.

Workforce Development as Economic Policy

When workforce strategies are tied to economic development policies, they become powerful engines for poverty reduction. For example:

- Encouraging investment in sectors that offer **quality**

jobs with benefits.

- Supporting regional job clusters to anchor local economies.
- Incentivizing employers to hire and train workers from disadvantaged backgrounds.

Call to Action for Leaders

- Conduct a workforce needs assessment in your region.
- Establish industry councils that meet regularly to align education and training with job openings.
- Advocate for public and private investment in upskilling initiatives.

Workforce development is not just about filling jobs—it's about shaping economies where prosperity is shared.

Part III –
Health,
Family, and
Community

Chapter 9 – Health & Wellness: Building the Physical and Mental Foundations for Prosperity

Why Health Is an Economic Issue

Health is not just a personal matter—it is a **core driver of economic stability**. Poor health limits productivity, drains household resources, and restricts educational attainment.

According to the **World Health Organization (WHO)**, every **$1 invested in health yields up to $4 in economic returns**, due to increased productivity, reduced healthcare costs, and a more resilient workforce. Yet in low-income communities, health disparities remain stark: limited access to care, higher rates of chronic illness, and untreated mental health conditions undermine the path to prosperity.

The Vicious Cycle of Poor Health and Poverty

Health and poverty reinforce each other in ways that can last generations:

- Poverty increases exposure to environmental hazards, poor nutrition, and unsafe working conditions.
- Illness reduces the ability to work, lowering household income.
- Low income limits access to preventive care, perpetuating illness.

Breaking this cycle requires leaders to address **both the social determinants of health**—such as housing, education, and nutrition—and direct access to healthcare.

Case Study: Thailand's Universal Coverage Scheme

Thailand introduced a universal healthcare system in 2002, providing comprehensive coverage for all citizens. This policy reduced catastrophic health expenditures for low-income households and contributed to significant reductions in poverty-related health disparities.

Mental Health: The Overlooked Factor

The **Lancet Commission on Global Mental Health** warns that untreated mental health issues cost the global economy **$1 trillion annually** in lost productivity. In poverty-affected areas, the stress of survival can lead to chronic anxiety, depression, and trauma—conditions rarely addressed in traditional poverty reduction programs.

Leaders must normalize mental health support as part of any comprehensive development strategy.

The Leadership Role in Health Equity

1. **Integrate Health into Economic Development** – Ensure workforce and education programs include wellness components.
2. **Advocate for Affordable Care Access** – Support policies that expand insurance coverage and reduce healthcare costs.
3. **Invest in Prevention** – Promote nutrition, physical activity, and disease prevention programs.

Global Examples of Health-Driven Poverty Reduction

- **Rwanda**: Community-based health insurance programs have increased healthcare coverage to over 90% of the population.
- **Brazil**: The Family Health Strategy sends teams of

doctors and nurses into underserved communities, improving preventive care and reducing hospitalizations.

- **New Zealand**: Integrated mental health services in schools and workplaces are improving educational and employment outcomes.

Health as a Productivity Multiplier

Healthy individuals are more likely to remain employed, pursue education, and contribute to their communities. Leaders must understand that **investing in health is investing in human capital**—and therefore in long-term economic growth.

Call to Action for Leaders

- Partner with healthcare providers to bring services directly into underserved communities.
- Incorporate mental health awareness and support into schools, workplaces, and community programs.
- Champion workplace wellness policies that support both physical and mental health.

A society cannot be prosperous if its people are not healthy. Health equity is not optional—it is foundational.

Chapter 10 – Empowering Parents: Building Family Stability as a Catalyst for Prosperity

Why Parenting Support Is a Poverty Reduction Strategy

The family unit is the **first economy** a child experiences. Parents shape a child's values, health, education, and aspirations—long before formal institutions intervene. When parents are empowered with knowledge, resources, and confidence, they create environments where children can thrive, and poverty cycles can be broken.

According to **UNICEF**, early childhood development programs that involve parents lead to **better school readiness, higher lifetime earnings, and lower crime rates** for children. In economic terms, every $1 invested in parent-focused interventions can yield up to $7 in long-term benefits.

The Generational Impact of Parental Empowerment

Poverty is often passed down because children inherit the limitations of their parents' circumstances—not just financially, but in mindset and opportunity. By strengthening parental capacity, leaders help rewrite the trajectory of entire families.

Parental empowerment means:

- **Financial literacy** – Teaching budgeting, saving, and debt management.
- **Educational advocacy** – Equipping parents to navigate school systems and advocate for their children.
- **Health and nutrition knowledge** – Promoting family wellness as a foundation for learning and productivity.

Case Study: Brazil's Criança Feliz Program

This home-visiting program supports parents in low-income households, teaching them how to stimulate early childhood development through play, nutrition, and learning activities. It has reached over **1 million families** and is credited with improving developmental outcomes in children under three years old.

Challenges Faced by Parents in Low-Income Communities

1. **Time Poverty** – Working multiple jobs leaves little time for involvement in a child's development.
2. **Access Gaps** – Limited exposure to parenting resources and early childhood programs.
3. **Generational Disconnection** – Parents who lack positive role models may struggle to build nurturing family environments.

The Leadership Role in Parental Empowerment

Leaders can strengthen families by:

1. **Embedding Parenting Education** – Include workshops in schools, community centers, and workplaces.
2. **Integrating Family Services** – Link health, education, and employment programs for whole-family impact.
3. **Advocating for Family-Friendly Policies** – Support

parental leave, flexible work schedules, and affordable childcare.

Global Examples of Family-Centered Approaches

- **Finland**: Universal parental leave and subsidized childcare enable both parents to participate in the workforce without sacrificing child development.
- **South Africa**: The *Family Strengthening Program* helps caregivers in high-poverty areas access resources, manage stress, and create stable home environments.
- **United States**: *Nurse-Family Partnership* pairs first-time mothers with nurses for regular home visits, improving maternal and child health outcomes.

Family Stability as a National Asset

Strong families build strong communities, and strong communities build resilient economies. Parental empowerment is not charity—it is **nation-building at its most fundamental level**.

Call to Action for Leaders

- Support programs that integrate parenting education with workforce and education initiatives.
- Advocate for laws that protect working parents and promote early childhood development.
- Measure program success by **family stability indicators**, not just individual outcomes.

When parents are strong, children are strong—and the cycle of poverty has a much harder time taking root.

Chapter 11 – Building & Sustaining Community Relationships: The Social Infrastructure of Prosperity

Why Social Capital Is as Valuable as Financial Capital

Economies thrive when communities thrive.

Strong community relationships—networks of trust, collaboration, and shared resources—act as a form of **social capital** that can accelerate poverty reduction. According to the **OECD**, communities with high levels of social trust report **better health outcomes, higher civic engagement, and stronger economic resilience**.

Social capital is more than friendliness—it's the infrastructure of relationships that makes resource-sharing, problem-solving, and collective action possible.

The Link Between Community Cohesion and Poverty Reduction

When people feel connected and supported, they are more

likely to:

- Share job opportunities and business referrals.
- Mobilize resources during crises.
- Advocate for local improvements together.

Conversely, communities fractured by mistrust or isolation often face greater economic stagnation, even when financial resources are available.

Case Study: Medellín, Colombia

Once known as one of the most dangerous cities in the world, Medellín transformed through investments not only in infrastructure but in **community connection**. Leaders built libraries, parks, and public spaces in marginalized neighborhoods, creating places for residents to gather, learn, and collaborate. The result: crime rates fell, local businesses grew, and the city became a model of inclusive urban development.

Challenges to Building Community Relationships in Poverty-Affected Areas

1. **Resource Competition** – Scarcity can create rivalry instead of cooperation.

2. **Mistrust of Institutions** – Historical neglect or exploitation can weaken engagement.
3. **High Mobility** – Frequent relocation for work or housing disrupts long-term bonds.

The Leadership Role in Strengthening Community Networks

Leaders can foster community relationships by:

1. **Creating Shared Spaces** – Parks, community centers, and markets where people connect naturally.
2. **Supporting Local Organizations** – Funding and mentoring grassroots initiatives.
3. **Facilitating Dialogue** – Encouraging conversations between diverse groups to build trust.

Global Examples of Social Capital in Action

- **Kenya**: The *Harambee* tradition—community fundraising for shared goals—has financed schools, businesses, and local infrastructure for decades.
- **Japan**: Neighborhood associations (*chonaikai*) coordinate disaster preparedness, festivals, and

community improvement projects.

- **Canada**: Community co-ops in rural areas pool resources for essential services like broadband internet and grocery stores.

Community as an Economic Multiplier

When communities are strong, they attract investment, retain talent, and inspire innovation. Social capital reduces the transaction costs of doing business—people are more willing to collaborate when trust is high.

Call to Action for Leaders

- Invest in community spaces that encourage interaction and collaboration.
- Support local leadership development to sustain community engagement.
- Measure community health through **trust and participation indicators** as well as economic metrics.

Communities with strong relationships are harder to break and easier to build upon—making them one of the most powerful weapons against poverty.

Chapter 12 – Sports, Education & Leadership: Harnessing the Power of Play for Social Mobility

Why Sports Are More Than Games

Sports are often seen as recreation—but for many individuals and communities, they are a **pathway to education, leadership, and opportunity**.

The **UN Inter-Agency Task Force on Sport for Development and Peace** recognizes sports as a cost-effective tool to achieve multiple Sustainable Development Goals, from quality education to gender equality to reduced inequalities.

In many low-income communities, sports can:

- Provide scholarships for higher education.
- Build discipline, teamwork, and leadership skills.
- Create career pathways in coaching, sports management, and related industries.

From the Playing Field to the Boardroom

Athletic participation teaches transferable skills highly valued in the workforce:

- **Teamwork** – Collaborating toward shared goals.
- **Strategic thinking** – Adapting quickly to changing situations.
- **Resilience** – Bouncing back from setbacks.

These are the same competencies leaders need to drive organizations and communities forward.

Case Study: Right to Play

Operating in over 15 countries, Right to Play uses sports and play-based learning to teach children life skills, improve academic performance, and promote gender equality. In participating communities, school attendance has increased by up to **80%**.

The Role of Sports in Education Access

For many students, sports scholarships are the gateway to higher education they might otherwise never afford. In the

United States alone, more than **180,000 student-athletes** receive sports scholarships annually. Globally, universities are increasingly integrating sports recruitment into international student programs.

Challenges in Leveraging Sports for Social Mobility

1. **Limited Access** – Rural and low-income areas often lack safe sports facilities and trained coaches.
2. **Overemphasis on Professional Careers** – Many youth see professional sports as the only goal, overlooking educational and leadership pathways.
3. **Gender Barriers** – Girls in some communities face cultural restrictions that limit participation.

The Leadership Role in Sports Development

Leaders can maximize the impact of sports on poverty reduction by:

1. **Integrating Sports with Education** – Ensure participation is tied to academic performance and life skills training.

2. **Investing in Facilities** – Build safe, accessible spaces for youth to play and train.

3. **Promoting Inclusive Participation** – Ensure girls, children with disabilities, and marginalized groups have equal access.

Global Examples of Sports as a Catalyst for Change

- **Kenya**: The Mathare Youth Sports Association combines soccer leagues with environmental clean-ups, HIV awareness, and leadership training.
- **Afghanistan**: Skateistan uses skateboarding to engage children in education, with a strong focus on empowering girls.
- **Brazil**: Favela Street trains young people from marginalized neighborhoods to become community sports leaders.

Sports as a Leadership Incubator

Sports often identify and develop leaders who might otherwise go unnoticed. Coaches, captains, and event organizers learn to motivate teams, resolve conflicts, and plan strategically—skills that transfer directly to civic and business leadership.

Call to Action for Leaders

- Partner with schools and clubs to integrate sports into broader education and development programs.

- Fund coaching and mentorship programs that connect athletics with career planning.
- Advocate for policies that protect and expand access to sports in underserved communities.

Sports are not just games—they are powerful platforms for education, leadership, and opportunity. Leaders who harness their potential can move individuals and entire communities from survival to success.

Part IV – Systems, Advocacy, and Wealth

Chapter 13 – Civic Engagement & Leadership: Mobilizing Communities for Policy and Change

Why Civic Engagement Is a Cornerstone of Poverty Reduction

Lasting change happens when communities have the power to influence the decisions that shape their lives.

Civic engagement—the active participation of citizens in public life—is a critical pathway for shifting policies, resources, and systems toward equity.

According to the **World Bank**, countries with high civic participation see **more responsive governance, better public services, and stronger economic growth**. In contrast, communities with low participation often experience underinvestment, policy neglect, and continued poverty.

From Participation to Leadership

Civic engagement is more than voting—it includes:

- Attending town halls and public hearings.

- Joining advisory boards and advocacy groups.
- Organizing petitions, campaigns, and community coalitions.

When individuals step from being passive observers to **active leaders**, they help steer policies toward poverty reduction and inclusive growth.

Case Study: Participatory Budgeting in Porto Alegre, Brazil

In the late 1980s, Porto Alegre pioneered participatory budgeting, allowing citizens—especially from low-income neighborhoods—to decide how public funds were spent. The result: increased investment in sanitation, health, and education in the poorest areas, and a dramatic rise in civic participation.

Barriers to Civic Engagement in Low-Income Communities

1. **Distrust of Government** – Often rooted in histories of neglect or exploitation.
2. **Lack of Awareness** – Many are unaware of opportunities to engage in decision-making.

3. **Time and Resource Constraints** – When survival consumes daily energy, civic participation can feel like a luxury.

The Leadership Role in Strengthening Civic Engagement

Leaders—whether in government, business, or civil society—can:

1. **Educate Citizens on Their Rights and Processes** – Provide accessible, multilingual information about participation opportunities.
2. **Facilitate Dialogue Between Communities and Institutions** – Build trust and transparency.
3. **Invest in Civic Leadership Development** – Train residents to navigate policy systems, lead advocacy efforts, and hold officials accountable.

Global Examples of Civic Leadership in Action

- **India**: The *Right to Information Act* has empowered rural communities to demand accountability in public spending.

- **United States**: Community organizing models pioneered by groups like the Industrial Areas Foundation have mobilized neighborhoods to secure housing, schools, and infrastructure improvements.
- **Tunisia**: Youth-led civic movements played a key role in democratic reforms after the Arab Spring.

Civic Engagement as a Poverty Disruptor

When communities engage civically, they can influence:

- Education funding and curriculum reforms.
- Housing policies that increase affordability.
- Labor laws that protect wages and working conditions.

Civic engagement changes the **power dynamics** that keep poverty in place—it shifts decision-making from being "done to" communities to being "done with" them.

Call to Action for Leaders

- Sponsor civic education workshops and leadership programs.

- Build partnerships between grassroots groups and policymakers.
- Track and share metrics on community participation and its outcomes.

A community that participates in its own governance builds not just policies—it builds power. And power is essential to breaking the cycle of poverty.

Chapter 14 – Financial Wealth Development: Turning Economic Gains into Generational Prosperity

Why Wealth, Not Just Income, Breaks the Poverty Cycle

Earning more money is important—but without the ability to **build and retain wealth**, communities remain vulnerable to economic shocks. Wealth provides a safety net, fuels investment in education and business, and creates the conditions for generational mobility.

According to the **Brookings Institution**, the median wealth gap between white and Black households in the U.S. is **nearly 8 to 1**. Globally, the **Credit Suisse Global Wealth Report** shows that the richest 10% of the population owns **76% of global wealth**, leaving billions with little or no assets. Closing these gaps requires deliberate, sustained wealth-building strategies.

The Difference Between Income and Wealth

- **Income** is money earned through work or investments.
- **Wealth** is the accumulation of assets—such as property, savings, and stocks—that generate future income.

Without wealth, a job loss, medical emergency, or economic downturn can erase years of progress. Wealth gives families **resilience**—the ability to weather storms without falling back into poverty.

From Financial Literacy to Financial Empowerment

Financial education alone is not enough—people need **access to tools and opportunities** to put that knowledge into practice. Effective wealth development strategies include:

- **Saving and Investment Programs** – Encouraging both short- and long-term asset growth.
- **Property Ownership** – Building equity through housing or land ownership.

- **Entrepreneurship and Business Equity** – Creating income-generating assets that appreciate over time.

Case Study: Singapore's Central Provident Fund (CPF)

Singapore mandates contributions from both employers and employees into a national savings system that can be used for housing, healthcare, and retirement. This has enabled the majority of citizens to own their homes and retire with financial security, even without high incomes.

Barriers to Wealth Development

1. **Low Financial Inclusion** – 1.4 billion adults globally remain unbanked (World Bank).
2. **Predatory Lending** – High-interest loans strip wealth from low-income communities.
3. **Lack of Inheritance Opportunities** – Many families start from zero each generation.

The Leadership Role in Wealth Development

Leaders can accelerate wealth building by:

1. **Expanding Access to Financial Services** – Support microfinance, mobile banking, and community credit unions.
2. **Promoting Asset Ownership** – Advocate for affordable housing programs and small business grants.
3. **Creating Investment Pathways** – Encourage participation in retirement plans, cooperatives, and stock ownership programs.

Global Examples of Wealth Development Initiatives

- **Kenya**: M-Pesa mobile banking has brought millions of unbanked citizens into the financial system.
- **Canada**: Registered Education Savings Plans (RESPs) help families save for children's higher education with government matching.
- **South Korea**: Government-backed savings accounts for low-income workers match contributions to

accelerate asset accumulation.

Wealth as a Tool for Equity

When wealth is concentrated in a few hands, inequality deepens. But when wealth is distributed more broadly, communities gain the **power to invest in their own future**, fund local initiatives, and pass on opportunities to the next generation.

Call to Action for Leaders

- Sponsor community investment and savings programs.
- Advocate for policies that protect consumers and promote asset ownership.
- Measure success not just by income growth, but by **net worth and asset accumulation**.

Income gets you through the month. Wealth gets you through generations. Leaders who focus on wealth development create prosperity that endures.

Chapter 15 – Cross-Sector Partnerships: Scaling Solutions Beyond Borders

Why Collaboration Is the New Currency of Leadership

No single sector—government, business, education, or civil society—possesses the resources or reach to eradicate poverty alone. Poverty is systemic, and systems can only be transformed when stakeholders align around shared goals.

The **World Economic Forum** underscores that cross-sector collaboration is central to achieving the **UN Sustainable Development Goals (SDGs)**, especially Goal 1: *No Poverty*. In practice, this means moving away from isolated efforts and toward partnerships that pool **capital, knowledge, networks, and influence**.

In today's interconnected world, collaboration is not just an option—it is the **currency of leadership**.

The Global Scale of Partnership Impact

Consider the complexity of poverty: it involves health, education, housing, finance, governance, and community.

Partnerships allow us to address these dimensions simultaneously.

- **Governments** bring scale, legitimacy, and policy leverage.
- **Private sector** brings efficiency, innovation, and investment capital.
- **Nonprofits and grassroots organizations** bring trust, local knowledge, and community mobilization.
- **International organizations** bring frameworks, resources, and global accountability.

When these forces align, **impact multiplies**—solutions scale faster, reach more people, and last longer.

Case Study: Gavi, the Vaccine Alliance

Since 2000, Gavi has brought together governments, pharmaceutical companies, foundations, and international agencies to deliver life-saving vaccines to low-income nations. The results are staggering:

- **981 million children immunized.**
- **16.2 million future deaths prevented.**
- Entire health systems strengthened through better logistics, technology, and infrastructure.

What makes Gavi powerful is not only the health outcomes—it's the model of partnership. By aligning diverse interests under a shared mission, Gavi proved that **global problems demand global alliances.**

Leadership Strategies for Building Partnerships

1. **Identify Shared Interests** – Focus on win-win outcomes for all sectors. For example, businesses benefit from healthier workforces, governments from reduced public health costs, and nonprofits from expanded reach.
2. **Establish Clear Accountability** – Define roles, metrics, and governance structures up front to avoid duplication or gaps.
3. **Leverage Collective Resources** – Share not only money, but also data, expertise, infrastructure, and influence.

Call to Action for Leaders

Ask yourself: *Are you building alliances that multiply your impact—or are you trying to solve complex challenges in isolation?*

The greatest leaders of the 21st century will not be those who solve problems alone, but those who build **coalitions strong enough to solve them together**.

Chapter 16 – Measuring What Matters: Impact, Accountability, and Legacy

Next Steps – From Vision to Action to Impact

The Work Is Urgent. The Work Is Possible.

Throughout this book, we've explored how poverty can be broken—not just managed—through leadership, innovation, and collaboration. The message is clear: poverty is not an inevitable condition; it is a challenge that can be dismantled with deliberate, sustained effort.

Across the globe, examples abound of communities transforming themselves when given the tools, resources, and opportunities to thrive. But transformation doesn't happen by accident. It happens when leaders—whether in business, government, education, or grassroots movements—step forward with **clarity of vision, courage in action, and commitment to lasting impact**.

The Vision to Action to Impact Framework in Practice

You now have a model that works anywhere—from rural villages to bustling cities:

- **Vision** – Imagine a future without poverty and define it with precision.
- **Action** – Build programs, policies, and partnerships that directly target barriers to prosperity.
- **Impact** – Measure changes not by temporary relief, but by generational outcomes.

This is not a linear process. Vision inspires action, action produces impact, and impact strengthens vision. Each stage fuels the next, creating a cycle of progress rather than a cycle of poverty.

The Leader's Mandate

The fight against poverty is **not charity—it is leadership at its highest level**.

Leaders in every sector have the power to:

- Redirect resources toward lasting change.

- Elevate marginalized voices in decision-making.
- Model ethical, inclusive, and sustainable growth.

Your mandate is to lead where you are, with what you have, and to leverage your influence to open doors for others.

Global Urgency, Local Action

While poverty is a global challenge—impacting more than **700 million people living on less than $2.15 a day** (World Bank)—solutions are most powerful when rooted in a local **context**. Leaders must adapt global best practices to local realities, ensuring that strategies resonate culturally, economically, and socially.

Your Next Steps

1. **Assess Your Sphere of Influence** – Identify where you can lead change right now.
2. **Choose One Area to Begin** – Whether it's workforce development, education, health, or entrepreneurship, start somewhere concrete.
3. **Build Partnerships** – Collaborate across sectors and geographies.
4. **Measure and Share Impact** – Inspire others by

showing what works.

An Invitation to Join the Movement

Breaking the cycle of poverty is not the work of a few heroic individuals—it is a collective mission. By committing to **turning vision into action, and action into impact**, you join a global community of leaders determined to replace poverty with prosperity.

The question is no longer **"Can it be done?"**
The question is **"Will you lead the way?"**

Because the next chapter in this story is not written by me—it's written by you.

From Global Perspective to Leadership Ownership

We've looked across the globe and seen what is possible when nations, institutions, and communities align their efforts. From Rwanda's healthcare reforms to Brazil's community empowerment programs, from Vietnam's multidimensional poverty model to Gavi's international partnerships—we know that poverty is not unbreakable.

But global progress, as inspiring as it is, will never be enough on its own. Systems only change when **individual leaders choose ownership**. The responsibility does not rest with governments or organizations alone—it rests with every leader who dares to see differently, act decisively, and measure relentlessly.

And this includes **aspiring leaders**—those still rising, still finding their voice. Because leadership is not defined by position; it is defined by responsibility. The future will not wait for you to feel ready. Transformation begins the moment you choose accountability and step into action.

The world does not need more managers of poverty—it needs transformational leaders who will own the challenge, embrace accountability, and drive the vision into impact.

Across continents, we've seen that poverty is not invincible. Rwanda's commitment to community healthcare, Brazil's neighborhood-based development, Vietnam's multidimensional poverty index, and Gavi's international partnerships all remind us that when vision, action, and accountability converge, transformation is possible at scale.

But here is the truth: global progress, as vital as it is, will never be enough. Poverty is not broken by statistics alone. It is broken when individual leaders choose to take ownership of the problem and see themselves as accountable for the solutions.

And leadership is not reserved for those with titles, budgets, or influence. **Aspiring leaders—students, community members, rising professionals—must see themselves as part of this mandate.** Leadership is defined not by position but by responsibility. Transformation begins the moment someone refuses to wait for permission and instead commits to action.

What the world needs now are not caretakers of poverty but **transformational leaders**—men and women who will own the challenge, embrace accountability, and commit to bold action. It is this shift—from global examples to personal ownership—that will turn possibility into reality.

Final Call – Ownership, Accountability, and Transformational Leadership

The Leadership Imperative

The journey from poverty to prosperity cannot rest on programs alone. It cannot rest solely on governments, nonprofits, or businesses. It rests on **leaders**—and not just the established leaders of today, but the aspiring leaders who will carry this work into tomorrow.

Leadership is not a position. Leadership is a **mandate**—to see clearly, to act boldly, and to measure impact honestly. Ownership is the first step: refusing to pass the responsibility to "someone else" or "someday." The moment a leader claims responsibility for change, the cycle of poverty begins to weaken.

Accountability as the Engine of Change

True leadership demands accountability. Not the kind that counts outputs—how many people were served, how many programs were launched—but the kind that measures outcomes: how many families are no longer trapped in poverty, how many communities have achieved stability, how many young people now inherit opportunity instead of disadvantage.

Accountability means leaders must answer the hard questions: Did we create lasting change? Did we build systems that endure beyond our tenure? Did we multiply leadership so others can continue the work?

Action that Transforms

Vision inspires. Accountability guides. But it is **action** that transforms.

Action means moving beyond talk, beyond planning, beyond good intentions. It means mobilizing people, resources, and influence with urgency. It means building partnerships that multiply impact instead of working in isolation. And it means making bold decisions that may be unpopular in the short term but transformational in the long term.

Transformational leadership is not about maintaining systems—it is about **redesigning them** so poverty no longer defines the future.

A Call to Leaders and Aspiring Leaders Alike

To the leaders already in positions of power: the world is waiting for you to step beyond management into transformation. Use your influence, your resources, and your platforms to dismantle systems that keep people trapped.

To the aspiring leaders: do not wait for permission. Leadership is not bestowed; it is chosen. Begin where you are, with what you have. Lead in your classroom, your workplace, your neighborhood. Your voice and your vision are needed now, not someday.

The Charge

This is the moment. Poverty will not be broken by accident—it will be broken by leaders who own the challenge, hold themselves accountable, and act with courage.

The future is asking a question of you:

- Will you manage poverty—or will you break it?
- Will you measure activity—or will you measure transformation?
- Will you lead for applause today—or for legacy tomorrow?

The tools are here. The frameworks are proven. The need is urgent.

The only missing ingredient is you.

Step forward. Lead boldly. And together, let us turn vision into action, and action into impact.

PART I: The Leadership Mandate: Answering the Call to Break Poverty

Chapter 1 – The Leadership Mandate: Owning the Fight Against Poverty

From Global Crisis to Personal Responsibility

The fight against poverty is not "someone else's" mission—it is ours. Yours. Mine. Ours collectively. The myth that poverty is the concern of governments, charities, or "specialized experts" has allowed millions of capable leaders to stand on the sidelines, believing their role is peripheral.

But here's the truth: **wherever you have influence, you have responsibility**. Whether you lead a team of three or a corporation of three thousand, whether you run a small farm in rural Kenya or a startup in Silicon Valley, your decisions ripple outward. They affect how resources are distributed, how opportunities are created, and how communities either rise or stagnate.

Poverty is not confined to one geography. It may wear different faces—rural deprivation in Appalachia, urban unemployment in Lagos, educational inequity in Mumbai— but its root dynamics are similar. And leaders, no matter their field, have both the reach and the tools to dismantle it.

Leadership as a Poverty-Breaking Force

Leadership is not just a title; it is a force that can accelerate or hinder progress. In the context of poverty, leadership does one of three things:

1. **Sustain the status quo** – Avoiding the issue, playing it safe, and making decisions that leave inequities intact.
2. **Manage the symptoms** – Implementing programs that alleviate immediate suffering but leave systemic barriers untouched.
3. **Break the cycle** – Using vision, strategy, and action to remove the root causes and create lasting opportunity.

The poverty-breaking leader commits to the third path, knowing it is harder, slower, and often less celebrated in the short term—but infinitely more rewarding and impactful in the long term.

The Five Commitments of a Poverty-Breaking Leader

To move from aspiration to real change, leaders must embrace five non-negotiable commitments:

1. **Clarity of Vision**

   Leaders must articulate a future where poverty is not the norm. This vision is not a vague dream—it is specific, measurable, and compelling enough to inspire both resources and people.

2. **Systemic Understanding**

   Addressing poverty means understanding its structural roots—economic policy, education systems, access to healthcare, cultural norms, and market barriers. Without this knowledge, efforts will remain surface-level.

3. **Courage to Disrupt**

   Real change often means challenging entrenched systems and mindsets. Poverty-breaking leaders are willing to disrupt comfort zones, knowing that transformation requires discomfort.

4. **Coalition Building**

   No leader can do it alone. The ability to unite businesses, governments, nonprofits, and communities around a shared goal is essential. Poverty is a multi-sector problem; it demands multi-sector solutions.

5. **Relentless Measurement**

   Leaders must measure what matters—not just how many people are served, but how many lives are permanently transformed. Metrics must reflect generational change, not just quarterly outputs.

Bridging Global Lessons and Local Realities

While the principles of leadership are universal, their application must be deeply contextual. A microcredit program that succeeds in rural Bangladesh may fail in inner-city Chicago if it ignores the cultural, political, and market realities of that environment.

The poverty-breaking leader learns from global examples without falling into the trap of copy-paste solutions. They adapt strategies to the realities of their own communities while maintaining the core principles of empowerment, sustainability, and dignity.

- **Global Lesson:** Rwanda's integrated governance and private sector reforms reduced poverty dramatically.
- **Local Application:** A city government elsewhere might replicate the *integration principle*—aligning education, housing, and employment policies—while tailoring it to local culture and economic conditions.

This adaptability is what turns global inspiration into local transformation.

Why This Mandate Cannot Wait

The longer leaders delay in addressing poverty's root causes, the more entrenched those causes become. Poverty is not static—it compounds. Children born into poverty are statistically more likely to remain there, and each generation carries forward the deficits of the last unless a leader steps in to break the chain.

By 2030, without accelerated action, hundreds of millions will still live in extreme poverty. But history shows that when leaders act boldly—aligning vision with action and measuring for true impact—the curve can bend quickly.

The mandate is clear: **if you lead, you have a role in ending poverty**. If you aspire to lead, you have an opportunity to shape a legacy that will outlive you.

Your Role, Your Reach, Your Responsibility

As you read this book, I encourage you to locate yourself within the fight against poverty:

- What influence do you hold right now—through your position, your network, your expertise, your resources?
- What part of the poverty cycle intersects most with your sphere—education, housing, employment, healthcare, policy?
- What steps can you take, starting today, to move from management to mastery, from relief to renewal?

In the chapters ahead, you will see how the **Vision** → **Action** → **Impact** framework is applied in different contexts—how leaders in diverse environments have turned bold ideas into measurable change.

You will be challenged to think bigger, act sooner, and measure deeper. Because the leadership mandate is not for a select few—it is for every person who can influence outcomes. And that means you.

Chapter 2 – Vision: Seeing Beyond the Present

Why Vision is the First and Greatest Act of Leadership

Every movement that has reshaped history began with a vision. Not a mere goal. Not a vague hope. But a vivid, detailed picture of a better reality—one compelling enough to disrupt the status quo and galvanize action.

When it comes to poverty, vision is the leader's starting line. Without it, we are left with scattered projects and disconnected efforts. With it, we gain a blueprint for transformation, one that can be shared, scaled, and sustained.

Poverty-breaking leaders understand that vision is not an accessory to leadership—it is the **engine**. It shapes priorities, attracts partners, and guides every decision. A weak vision drains energy and resources. A strong vision becomes a magnet for people and ideas.

The Anatomy of a Poverty-Breaking Vision

A powerful vision has four defining qualities:

1. **Clarity** – It is concrete enough that people can imagine it clearly.
2. **Boldness** – It does not simply improve the present; it redefines what is possible.
3. **Credibility** – It is ambitious yet grounded in an understanding of what it will take to achieve it.
4. **Inclusivity** – It invites people from different walks of life to see themselves in the outcome.

When you say your vision out loud, people should not only believe it can happen—they should want to help make it happen.

Case Study 1: Medellín, Colombia – Reimagining a City

In the 1980s and '90s, Medellín was known as the world's most dangerous city, plagued by poverty and violence. The vision that sparked its transformation was radical: to become **"the most innovative city in the world."**

The leadership team's vision was not limited to crime reduction—it encompassed education, transportation, public spaces, and cultural identity. By painting a clear picture of what Medellín could become, they inspired unprecedented investment and citizen engagement.

The result? Between 2002 and 2012, the homicide rate dropped by over 80%, poverty fell dramatically, and the city became a global model for urban renewal.

Lesson for Leaders: A transformative vision must address more than the obvious problem; it must reimagine the entire ecosystem.

Case Study 2: Vision 2020 – Rwanda's National Transformation

After the devastation of the 1994 genocide, Rwanda's leadership articulated **Vision 2020**—a national plan to become a middle-income country within a generation.

The vision included governance reform, infrastructure investment, universal education, and private sector growth. It wasn't a slogan—it was a measurable, time-bound commitment.

By aligning government, business, and civil society behind a single picture of the future, Rwanda cut poverty rates from 77% in 1994 to 55% by 2017 and significantly improved health and education outcomes.

Lesson for Leaders: A vision gains power when it is measurable, time-bound, and owned by every sector.

Case Study 3: Grameen Bank – Financial Inclusion for the Poorest

In rural Bangladesh, millions of women had no access to credit, trapping them in cycles of poverty. Muhammad Yunus envisioned something audacious: a bank that would lend to the poorest, without collateral, trusting in their capacity to repay and build businesses.

That vision became Grameen Bank, which has provided microloans to millions, with repayment rates consistently above 95%. Women used these loans to start businesses, send their children to school, and break free from generational poverty.

Lesson for Leaders: A powerful vision reframes the problem—not as "how do we help the poor?" but as "how do we unleash their potential?"

Building Your Own Vision: A Leader's Blueprint

To craft a poverty-breaking vision for your context, ask yourself:

- **What future do I see that does not yet exist?** Be specific—paint the picture in detail.

- **Who benefits, and how will their lives change?**
  Ground it in human outcomes, not just statistics.
- **What barriers must be dismantled?** Name them
  clearly; avoidance dilutes credibility.
- **What values will guide the journey?** Vision without
  values can win the wrong kind of support.
- **What time horizon makes sense?** A vision without a
  timeline is a wish.

Write it down. Speak it often. Test it in conversations with
those inside and outside your circle. A vision grows stronger
through dialogue

From Vision to Alignment

Once a vision is set, the leader's next role is alignment—
ensuring that every initiative, every partnership, and every
investment serves that vision. This is where many leaders
falter: they craft inspiring visions but fail to connect daily
actions to the larger goal.

In Medellín, every infrastructure project—from cable cars to
libraries—was tied back to the vision of an innovative city. In
Rwanda, every policy was assessed against Vision 2020
benchmarks. In Bangladesh, every loan reinforced the belief
in human capacity.

A vision without alignment is like a compass without a map—it points somewhere, but you'll never arrive. 💾

A Challenge to the Reader

As you finish this chapter, I challenge you to put your vision on paper.

Make it:

- So clear that a 12-year-old could explain it.
- So bold that it scares you a little.
- So credible that you can identify the first three steps toward it.
- So inclusive that people from different sectors see themselves in it.

Chapter 3 – Action: Turning Vision into Measurable Progress

Why Action Is the True Test of Leadership

Vision, no matter how inspiring, changes nothing until it is acted upon.

A well-crafted vision can attract attention, spark conversations, and even secure commitments—but without disciplined execution, it remains a beautifully framed picture of a future that never comes to life.

This is where many leaders falter—not because they lack passion, but because the leap from big-picture aspiration to ground-level implementation feels daunting. In this stage, leadership moves from *what you see* to *what you do*.

Action is the crucible in which leaders prove their seriousness. It demands strategy, courage, and persistence, because turning vision into reality is rarely smooth or linear.

The Three Pillars of Action in Poverty-Breaking Leadership

1. **Strategic Planning: From Vision to Roadmap**
   - Break down your vision into milestones.

- Identify which actions will create the greatest leverage—small shifts that produce large results.
- Align resources with priorities; avoid spreading efforts too thin.

2. **Partnership Building: Expanding Reach and Resources**
   - Poverty is multi-dimensional; solving it requires multi-sector collaboration.
   - Identify potential allies across government, private sector, civil society, and grassroots networks.
   - Approach partnerships as co-ownership, not charity; every partner must see mutual value.

3. **Rapid Prototyping: Testing Before Scaling**
   - Pilot small-scale initiatives to test ideas in real conditions.
   - Gather feedback from beneficiaries and partners; adjust quickly.
   - Use early wins to build momentum and credibility before expanding.

Case Study 1: Medellín's Integrated Transport System

In Chapter 2, we saw Medellín's bold vision to become the most innovative city in the world. The real change came when leaders **acted**—connecting marginalized hillside communities to the city's economic hub through cable cars, escalators, and new public spaces.

These were not symbolic gestures; they were targeted actions that directly linked residents to jobs, schools, and services. The projects were tested in phases, then expanded, ensuring community trust and consistent progress.

Lesson for Leaders: Prioritize actions that directly dismantle barriers and link people to opportunity.

Case Study 2: India's Rural Solar Electrification

In regions of rural India where electricity was unreliable or nonexistent, the vision was universal energy access. The action plan involved small-scale solar grids installed by local entrepreneurs trained and financed through microloans.

The model was piloted in a few villages, refined based on local conditions, and scaled nationally. The result: thousands of communities gained consistent power, improving education, health services, and economic productivity.

Lesson for Leaders: Combine technical solutions with local ownership for long-term sustainability. 🗒

From Action Lists to Action Culture

Many organizations create action lists; fewer create **action cultures**—environments where forward movement is embedded in the DNA of the team.

To build an action culture:

- Set short, achievable deadlines alongside long-term goals.
- Celebrate progress publicly to maintain momentum.
- Address bottlenecks quickly; do not let small obstacles stall major initiatives.
- Keep decision-making as close to the ground as possible; empower those directly involved to adapt and act.

An action culture thrives when leaders balance urgency with patience—moving quickly enough to maintain energy, but steadily enough to ensure lasting results.

Overcoming the Three Enemies of Action

1. **Perfectionism** – Waiting for the perfect plan stalls progress. Leaders must act with the information they have, adapting as they go.
2. **Fear of Failure** – In poverty-breaking work, some ideas will fail. Treat failure as feedback, not defeat.
3. **Fragmentation** – When actions aren't coordinated, efforts lose power. Align every project with the overarching vision.

Measuring as You Move

In the action phase, measurement is not an afterthought—it's a steering wheel. Without it, you can move quickly in the wrong direction.

- Establish **clear indicators** tied to your vision.
- Measure both outputs (services delivered) and outcomes (lives changed).
- Use data to refine, not just to report.

In Rwanda's Vision 2020, quarterly reviews measured progress across education, health, and economic indicators, allowing for rapid course correction when targets slipped.

The Leadership Shift: From Dreamer to Builder

Action transforms a leader's identity. You are no longer just the one who paints the future—you become the one who builds it.

This shift requires:

- Steadiness under pressure.
- Willingness to make unpopular decisions if they serve the vision.
- Relentless follow-through, even when enthusiasm fades.

The poverty-breaking leader accepts that execution is the unglamorous, often grueling part of the journey—but it is also the part where lives change.

A Challenge to the Reader

By the end of this week:

- Identify one action that directly advances your vision.
- Decide who else needs to be involved to make it happen.
- Set a clear deadline for the first milestone.

Small, strategic steps taken consistently will always outperform large plans that never leave the page.

Chapter 4 – Impact: Measuring What Truly Matters

Impact as the Leader's Legacy

Vision inspires. Action moves.

But **impact**—sustained, measurable change—is the only thing that proves leadership has made a real difference.

Too many leaders stop at activity reports: "We trained 500 people. We distributed 10,000 meals. We built 50 houses." These are outputs, not outcomes. They measure what was done, not what was changed.

The poverty-breaking leader holds a higher standard: *How many people no longer need our help? How many communities have moved from dependence to independence? How many systems have been restructured so they will not recreate poverty?*

Impact is not the end of leadership—it is the leader's legacy.

Defining True Impact

True impact is not only **visible** but **durable**. It changes the trajectory of lives and communities for years to come.

A program that trains unemployed youth for six months is a good start. But if, five years later, those youth are still employed, earning higher wages, and mentoring the next generation, that is **impact**.

True impact has three qualities:

1. **Sustainability** – The change persists without constant outside intervention.
2. **Scalability** – The model can be expanded or replicated in other contexts.
3. **Systemic Influence** – The work changes structures, not just circumstances.

Case Study 1: Vietnam's Holistic Poverty Reduction Program

Vietnam's national poverty strategy did not stop at raising incomes—it tracked progress in education, health, housing stability, and access to clean water.

By measuring across multiple dimensions, the program ensured that gains in one area weren't undermined by setbacks in another. Over 20 years, the country cut poverty rates by more than half, with corresponding improvements in literacy, child nutrition, and infrastructure.

Lesson for Leaders: Impact is strongest when it's multidimensional.

Case Study 2: Brazil's Bolsa Família Program

Bolsa Família provided conditional cash transfers to low-income families, but its impact came from linking payments to school attendance and health checkups. Over time, school completion rates rose, child malnutrition declined, and poverty rates fell dramatically.

By tying short-term relief to long-term capacity building, the program ensured that immediate benefits translated into generational change.

Lesson for Leaders: Design interventions that produce both immediate relief and future resilience.

From Data to Decisions

Many leaders measure for the sake of reporting to donors or boards. Poverty-breaking leaders measure for **learning**. They treat data as a steering wheel, not a rearview mirror.

Three steps for leaders to measure impact effectively:

1. **Set Indicators That Matter** – Go beyond outputs to track education levels, job retention, health improvements, or business growth.
2. **Collect Data Regularly** – Quarterly or semi-annual tracking ensures timely course corrections.
3. **Close the Loop** – Use findings to refine programs, adjust strategies, or end initiatives that are not working.

This approach prevents the common trap of continuing programs that feel good but don't produce lasting change.

The Risk of Mistaking Activity for Impact

In the leadership space, there is a temptation to showcase busyness as effectiveness—press releases, events, photo opportunities. These may create visibility, but visibility without impact is an empty victory.

True impact is often quieter. It shows up in reduced dependency, increased self-sufficiency, and shifts in community norms. The leader's role is to resist the lure of short-term applause in favor of long-term transformation.

Building an Impact Culture

Just as Chapter 3 emphasized creating an *action culture*, leaders must also cultivate an *impact culture*:

- Every team member understands what success looks like.
- Decision-making is guided by evidence, not just enthusiasm.
- Failures are acknowledged and used as learning tools.
- Celebrations highlight results, not just activity.

An impact culture ensures that an organization never loses sight of why it exists in the first place.

Case Study 3: The Graduation Approach

Used in multiple countries, the Graduation Approach combines asset transfers (like livestock or seed capital), skills training, and coaching. Its impact is measured not at the end of the program, but years later—when participants are still earning steady incomes, have savings, and are participating in community decision-making.

Follow-up studies show lasting improvements in economic security and social inclusion, proving that multi-faceted interventions can break poverty cycles for good.

Lesson for Leaders: Design for the long game; measure beyond the program timeline.

The Leader's Responsibility in the Impact Stage

At the impact stage, the leader's role evolves from builder to steward. It is no longer about proving you can deliver—it is about ensuring the delivery creates a legacy of independence, dignity, and opportunity.

The poverty-breaking leader asks constantly:

- Is this change sticking?
- Is it spreading?
- Is it changing the system, so it doesn't need to be repeated?

Only when the answer to all three is "yes" can we claim victory.

A Challenge to the Reader

As you think about your own leadership:

- Identify one area where you are currently measuring **activity** but not **impact**.
- Define what lasting success would look like there.

- Commit to tracking it over the next 12–24 months.

Because in the end, leaders are remembered not for what they started, but for what they finished—and what endured.

Chapter 5 – Leading Beyond Yourself: Securing a Legacy of Change

Why Leadership That Lasts Must Outlive the Leader

Every leader will one day step aside—by choice or by circumstance. The test of poverty-breaking leadership is not only *what happens while you are in the role* but *what continues after you are gone.*

Too many initiatives rise and fall with the person who championed them. When that leader leaves, the vision loses momentum, partnerships dissolve, and systems revert to old patterns. This is not just a loss of progress—it is a betrayal of the communities we serve.

Poverty-breaking leadership demands that we build **structures, cultures, and successors** capable of sustaining the work long after our departure.

The Three Anchors of Leadership Continuity

1. **Systems, Not Just Heroes**

- A leader's greatest achievement is to make themselves less necessary over time.
- Build decision-making processes, funding mechanisms, and accountability systems that function without constant intervention.
- Codify methods, partnerships, and policies so they are not dependent on memory or personality.

2. **Successor Development**
   - Identify and mentor emerging leaders early.
   - Give them opportunities to lead projects, manage resources, and represent the organization externally.
   - Ensure they inherit not just authority, but the *values* and *strategic clarity* that guide the work.

3. **Cultural Embedding**
   - Create a culture where the mission is so ingrained that new leaders feel compelled to carry it forward.
   - Align hiring, training, and performance reviews to reinforce this culture.
   - Celebrate milestones as collective achievements, not personal victories.

Case Study 1: The BRAC Model, Bangladesh

BRAC, one of the world's largest development organizations, has thrived through multiple leadership transitions because it institutionalized its approach. Programs are built on replicable systems, and leadership is intentionally distributed across layers of management.

When its founder Fazle Hasan Abed retired, the organization didn't falter—because the mission, values, and operating model were embedded in every corner of the institution.

Lesson for Leaders: Build organizations that can survive—and thrive—without their founders.

Case Study 2: Nelson Mandela and the South African Transition

Mandela's leadership was transformative, but his greatest act of service was preparing South Africa for leadership beyond himself. He chose to serve only one term as president, ensuring a peaceful transfer of power and reinforcing the principle that no one person is indispensable.

Lesson for Leaders: Sometimes the most powerful legacy is proving that leadership is bigger than the leader.

Building Leadership Multiplication into Your Impact Model

Legacy is not about cloning yourself—it's about multiplying leadership capacity so that the mission advances in ways you could not have imagined alone.

Practical steps:

- **Document and Share Knowledge** – Make playbooks, training modules, and process maps widely accessible.
- **Decentralize Authority** – Empower decision-making at multiple levels so leadership is distributed.
- **Institutionalize Learning** – Build feedback loops that survive leadership changes, ensuring continuous improvement.

When leadership is multiplied, your influence compounds far beyond your tenure.

Avoiding the Founder's Trap

Some leaders, especially in grassroots or entrepreneurial settings, fall into the "founder's trap": holding onto every decision, resisting change, or believing that no one else can lead as well.

This mindset, while understandable, is dangerous—it limits innovation, discourages emerging leaders, and makes the work fragile.

A poverty-breaking leader resists this trap by:

- Welcoming new ideas that challenge their own.
- Inviting diverse leadership styles.
- Recognizing that true legacy is measured in what endures without you.

The Emotional Side of Letting Go

Transitioning leadership is not only strategic—it is emotional. Leaders often feel a deep attachment to the work, fearing it will lose quality or integrity without them.

To navigate this:

- **Shift Identity** – See yourself as a builder of movements, not the movement itself.
- **Stay Connected, Not Controlling** – Remain a supporter or advisor without overshadowing new leadership.
- **Celebrate the Continuation** – Take pride in the fact that your absence is proof of your success in building sustainability.

A Challenge to the Reader

Ask yourself:

- If I left tomorrow, what would continue exactly as it is?
- What would collapse?
- Who is ready to lead, and what do they still need from me to succeed?

Identify one concrete step you can take this month to strengthen your organization, network, or initiative so that it thrives beyond your tenure.

Closing Thoughts

The mark of a poverty-breaking leader is not how indispensable they are, but how unnecessary they become—because the work is strong enough to stand without them. The greatest compliment you can receive is this: "They built something that lasts."

Next: We will move into **Part II of the book: The Leader's Toolkit,** beginning with **Chapter 6 – The Power of Cross-Sector Collaboration**—where we break down how to unite governments, businesses, nonprofits, and communities into one unstoppable force for poverty eradication.

Part II – The Leader's Toolkit: Strategies to Break Poverty's Grip

Chapter 6 – The Power of Cross-Sector Collaboration

Why Collaboration Is the Force Multiplier in Poverty Solutions

Poverty is not a single-issue problem. It touches education, health, housing, employment, finance, infrastructure, and governance—all at once. No single leader, organization, or sector has the reach, resources, or expertise to address all these dimensions alone.

That's why the leaders who make the deepest dents in poverty are those who **think beyond their own sector**—building alliances between governments, businesses, nonprofits, academia, and community networks. When done well, cross-sector collaboration creates *force multipliers*—solutions that move faster, cost less, and reach farther than any single player could achieve alone.

The Collaboration Gap

Many leaders acknowledge the need for collaboration but struggle to make it work. Common barriers include:

- **Mistrust** from past failed partnerships.

- **Competing agendas** that dilute focus.
- **Unequal power dynamics** that sideline community voices.
- **Short-term funding** that undermines long-term plans.

Poverty-breaking leaders navigate these barriers by creating partnerships grounded in shared goals, mutual benefit, and transparent accountability.

Three Principles of High-Impact Collaboration

1. **Mutual Value, Not One-Sided Charity**
   - Partnerships fail when one party sees itself as the "giver" and the other as the "receiver."
   - True collaboration is co-ownership: each partner gains value—whether that's social impact, market growth, political capital, or community trust.
2. **Clear, Shared Outcomes**
   - Vague agreements lead to scattered results.
   - Define success together, with metrics that matter to all partners.
3. **Equal Seats at the Table**
   - Include grassroots and community leaders alongside institutional partners.

- o Their lived experience shapes solutions that
  are relevant and sustainable.

Case Study 1: Skills Future, Singapore

Singapore's SkillsFuture program is a national skills
development initiative that unites government agencies,
employers, training providers, and industry associations. The
shared goal: equip every Singaporean with lifelong learning
opportunities to remain employable in a shifting economy.

Key to success: Each partner had a defined role. The
government provided funding and policy support, businesses
identified skill gaps, and training providers delivered
customized programs. The collaboration has strengthened
workforce resilience and reduced structural unemployment.

Lesson for Leaders: Align resources to specific, measurable
contributions from each sector.

Case Study 2: Clean Water Coalitions in Kenya

In Kenya, a coalition of local NGOs, government agencies,
engineering firms, and village councils tackled chronic water
scarcity. Businesses provided filtration technology, NGOs

managed training and education, government streamlined permits, and community leaders ensured cultural fit.

The result: Sustainable water systems installed in dozens of rural communities, maintained locally with minimal outside intervention.

Lesson for Leaders: Long-term success depends on both technical expertise and local stewardship.

Designing Your Own Cross-Sector Collaboration

Step 1 – Map the Ecosystem

Identify every stakeholder with a connection to the issue—direct or indirect. Include unlikely allies, such as financial institutions, media, or religious organizations.

Step 2 – Find the Overlap

Discover where your goals intersect. The sweet spot is where multiple parties see shared benefit from a single initiative.

Step 3 – Define Roles Clearly

Avoid role confusion by clarifying responsibilities and deliverables at the outset.

Step 4 – Establish Accountability

Set up mechanisms—regular reporting, public updates, joint evaluations—that keep all parties aligned.

Step 5 – Share Credit Generously

When collaboration succeeds, celebrate everyone's role. This strengthens trust for future partnerships.

The Leadership Skills Collaboration Requires

Cross-sector work challenges leaders to expand their skill set:

- **Negotiation** – balancing different priorities without diluting impact.
- **Translation** – bridging the language of business, policy, nonprofit missions, and community needs.
- **Patience and Persistence** – collaborations often move slower at first, but scale faster once trust is built.

A Challenge to the Reader

Choose one issue tied to your vision where your current approach would benefit from cross-sector collaboration. Ask yourself:

- Who in another sector could help us scale faster or solve more deeply?
- What value could I offer them in return?
- What would a joint success look like in measurable terms?

Take one step this month to initiate that conversation. Because when leaders work across boundaries, poverty has fewer places to hide.

Chapter 7 – Designing Solutions With, Not For, Communities

Why Co-Creation Outperforms Top-Down Design

One of the most common mistakes in poverty-related leadership is assuming that **expertise equals understanding**. You can have the best technical knowledge, the strongest funding base, and the most experienced team—but if solutions are designed *for* communities instead of *with* them, they will almost always fall short.

Why? Because communities understand the nuances of their own challenges and the cultural, economic, and social dynamics that shape them. Solutions that ignore these realities may look perfect on paper but fail in practice.

Co-creation isn't just ethical—it's **strategic**. It increases adoption, reduces resistance, and builds the capacity of communities to continue the work long after the initial intervention.

The Pitfalls of the "Parachute Approach"

In the "parachute approach," well-meaning leaders or organizations drop into a community, implement their idea, and leave—often without local input. The result:

- Infrastructure that isn't maintained because no one was trained to repair it.
- Programs that are culturally mismatched and quickly abandoned
- Mistrust toward outsiders, making future partnerships harder to build.

Poverty-breaking leaders reject this approach. Instead, they start by **listening before leading.**

Three Principles of Community Co-Creation

1. **Start with Questions, Not Answers**
   - Engage community members early to identify priorities from their perspective.
   - Ask: "What does success look like to you?" and "What has been tried before?"
2. **Share Power, Not Just Responsibility**
   - Ensure communities have decision-making authority, not just "input."

o This means budgeting with them, not just for them.

3. **Build Capacity, Not Dependency**
   o Every step of the solution should increase the community's ability to manage, adapt, and sustain the work without external leadership.

Case Study 1: Participatory Budgeting in Brazil

In Porto Alegre, Brazil, citizens directly decide how to allocate part of the municipal budget. Community assemblies determine priorities—schools, roads, health centers—and funds are distributed accordingly.

The result: Higher infrastructure quality, greater trust in government, and more equitable distribution of resources.

Lesson for Leaders: When communities control resources, they invest in what matters most to them.

Case Study 2: Farmer-Led Irrigation in East Africa

In several East African nations, NGOs shifted from building irrigation systems for farmers to training farmers to design, install, and maintain them.

Not only did adoption rates increase, but innovations emerged—farmers adapted the systems for local soil conditions and water sources, leading to higher yields and lower costs.

Lesson for Leaders: Communities often improve on external ideas when given the tools and trust to do so.

A Leader's Guide to Co-Creation

Step 1 – Listen Deeply
Spend time in the community without an agenda. Use surveys, focus groups, and informal conversations to understand needs and aspirations.

Step 2 – Map Local Assets
Identify existing skills, resources, and networks within the community. Build on what's already strong instead of starting from zero.

Step 3 – Co-Design Solutions
Bring together community members and external experts to brainstorm, prototype, and refine ideas.

Step 4 – Share Ownership
Ensure agreements are in writing—who owns the project,

who maintains it, and how decisions will be made in the future.

Step 5 – Exit Strategically

If external support is temporary, plan a gradual exit while strengthening local capacity to carry the work forward.

The Mindset Shift Leaders Must Make

Co-creation requires humility. It demands that leaders shift from being **solution providers** to **solution enablers**. This can feel slower at the start—but it accelerates sustainability in the long run.

It also requires cultural intelligence—understanding norms, communication styles, and decision-making patterns that differ from your own.

A Challenge to the Reader

Think about a project you lead or support:

- Who from the community has actual decision-making authority?

- How often do you listen without trying to fix immediately?

- What skills or systems could you transfer to ensure they don't need you in the future?

Make one adjustment this month to shift your approach from designing *for* to designing *with*.

Chapter 8 – Unlocking Economic Mobility Through Skills and Access

Why Economic Mobility Is the Real Poverty Breaker

Charity can relieve immediate suffering. Safety nets can prevent total collapse. But only **economic mobility**—the ability to improve one's income, stability, and quality of life over time—can permanently break the cycle of poverty.

Economic mobility is not just about earning more money; it's about gaining the **skills, opportunities, and networks** that allow individuals and communities to shape their own futures. Without it, people remain one setback away from the crisis.

For leaders, this means shifting from a mindset of *helping people survive* to *equipping people to thrive*.

The Three Levers of Economic Mobility

1. **Skills That Match the Market**
   - Training must align with actual economic demand, not just generic "employability."

- Digital literacy, problem-solving, and technical competencies are increasingly non-negotiable.
- Skills must be adaptable, so workers can pivot as industries change.

2. **Access to Opportunity**
   - Even the most skilled individuals can stagnate without access to jobs, capital, or markets.
   - Barriers—geographic, financial, social—must be identified and dismantled.
   - Access also means inclusion in decision-making and visibility to potential employers or investors.

3. **Networks That Open Doors**
   - Professional and social networks often determine who gets opportunities.
   - Leaders must intentionally connect underrepresented talent to influencers, mentors, and industry insiders.

Case Study 1: Germany's Dual Vocational Training System

Germany pairs classroom instruction with on-the-job apprenticeships, co-designed by industry and educational institutions. This ensures that skills taught match real labor market needs, leading to high employment rates among graduates.

Lesson for Leaders: Skills programs work best when employers are deeply involved in their design and delivery.

Case Study 2: Digital Skilling in Rural India

In rural India, organizations like Pratham and NASSCOM Foundation have introduced low-cost digital literacy and coding programs for youth, connecting graduates to remote work and freelance opportunities.

By combining skills training with market access (through job placement networks), thousands of young people moved from informal labor into sustainable digital careers.

Lesson for Leaders: Technology can bypass geographic limitations—if training is tied directly to income-generating opportunities.

From Skills to Systems

Skills training is only as effective as the **systems** that support graduates after they complete a program. Poverty-breaking leaders ensure that:

- Employers are ready to hire or contract trained workers.

- Financial institutions offer small loans or credit to those starting businesses.

- Mentors and peer networks provide guidance through the early stages of career or enterprise growth.

Without these systems, skills training risks becoming another dead-end intervention.

The Leadership Role in Unlocking Access

Leaders can use their influence to:

- Negotiate with employers to hire from marginalized communities.

- Advocate for policy changes that reduce licensing barriers or discriminatory hiring practices.

- Create platforms—online or offline—where talent and opportunity meet.

Sometimes the most impactful thing a leader can do is open a door that has been closed for decades.

Case Study 3: Peru's Artisan Export Network

In Peru, rural women artisans were trained in business skills and connected to global markets through a fair-trade export network. Sales tripled in three years, and income stability allowed families to invest in education and healthcare.

Lesson for Leaders: Market access can multiply the value of skills—turning craftsmanship into a sustainable livelihood.

Designing Your Own Economic Mobility Strategy

Step 1 – Identify Growth Sectors

Where is economic opportunity growing in your region or sector? Focus on industries with long-term demand.

Step 2 – Co-Design Training with Employers

Ensure skills are relevant from day one. Let employers help shape curriculum and commit to hiring graduates.

Step 3 – Build an Access Bridge

Create pathways—job boards, internship programs, buyer networks—that connect graduates to real opportunities.

Step 4 – Strengthen Support Systems

Pair skill-building with financial literacy, mentorship, and access to capital.

A Challenge to the Reader

Ask yourself:

- Are my current programs creating **skills, access,** and **networks**—or just one of the three?

- Which barrier (skills, access, networks) is most limiting in my context?
- What partner could I bring in to strengthen that weak link?

Take one concrete step this month to either align your skills training with market demand, remove an access barrier, or expand a network for someone who needs it.

Chapter 9 – Financing Change: Innovative Models for Sustainable Impact

Why Funding Models Make or Break Poverty Solutions

Even the most visionary plan will stall without the resources to execute it. But in poverty-related work, funding is often unpredictable—tied to donor cycles, seasonal giving, or political will. This instability forces leaders to focus on short-term fixes rather than long-term transformation.

Poverty-breaking leaders know that **how** you finance a solution is as important as the solution itself. The goal is not just to secure funding—it's to create **sustainable, diversified revenue streams** that outlast individual projects, leaders, or donors.

The Limitations of Traditional Funding

- **Donor Dependence** – Grants and charitable donations can create vulnerability when funders change priorities.

- **Short-Term Mindset** – Annual budget cycles often prioritize visible wins over deep, systemic change.

- **Restricted Funding** – Earmarked funds limit flexibility to adapt or innovate in response to new challenges.

To break poverty sustainably, leaders must look beyond the charity model toward **investment-oriented, self-sustaining financing approaches**.

Four Innovative Models for Sustainable Impact

1. **Social Enterprise Models**
   - Generate revenue by selling products or services that advance your mission.
   - Example: A vocational training center that funds its operations by selling goods produced by trainees.
   - Benefit: Reduces reliance on donations while reinforcing program goals.

2. **Impact Investing**
   - Investors provide capital to ventures that deliver measurable social and financial returns.

- Example: Affordable housing projects that generate rental income while improving living conditions.
- Benefit: Aligns investor interest with long-term community benefit.

3. **Blended Finance**
   - Combines public, private, and philanthropic capital to de-risk investments in underserved areas.
   - Example: A renewable energy project in sub-Saharan Africa financed by a mix of government grants, private loans, and NGO contributions.
   - Benefit: Leverages different types of capital to make high-impact projects viable.

4. **Community-Owned Funds**
   - Pooled resources managed by local stakeholders to finance ongoing initiatives.
   - Example: Village savings and loan associations that fund microenterprises.
   - Benefit: Builds local ownership and keeps economic benefits in the community.

Case Study 1: Grameen Shakti, Bangladesh

Grameen Shakti sells solar home systems to rural households using microloans. Revenue from sales sustains operations, while households save money by replacing kerosene with solar energy.

Lesson for Leaders: Financing models can simultaneously solve social problems and generate self-sustaining income streams.

Case Study 2: The Green Bond Movement

Cities like Johannesburg and Paris have issued "green bonds" to finance environmentally sustainable infrastructure. These bonds attract institutional investors while funding projects that improve long-term resilience—such as energy-efficient public housing that reduces costs for low-income residents.

Lesson for Leaders: Innovative finance tools can bring large-scale capital to community-focused goals.

Designing a Sustainable Funding Strategy

Step 1 – Assess Current Revenue Mix

What percentage of your budget comes from donations,

grants, earned income, or investments? Diversify to reduce risk.

Step 2 – Identify Income-Generating Opportunities
Look for ways to monetize existing assets, skills, or services without compromising mission integrity.

Step 3 – Build Investor-Ready Proposals
For impact investors and blended finance partners, focus on ROI in both social and financial terms.

Step 4 – Involve the Community in Financing
Local ownership increases accountability and long-term stability.

Overcoming the Fear of "Profit" in Social Change

Some leaders hesitate to embrace revenue generation, fearing it will dilute their mission. In reality, **financial sustainability amplifies mission impact**—because it allows you to scale and adapt without constant fundraising.

The key is **mission alignment**: Every revenue stream should reinforce, not distract from, your poverty-breaking objectives.

A Challenge to the Reader

Ask yourself:

- If all current donors withdrew tomorrow, what would keep my work alive?
- Which innovative financing model could I pilot in the next 12 months?
- Who could I partner with—inside or outside my sector—to bring that model to life?

Choose one small, concrete financing experiment to start now. Every sustainable funding source you build today is one less vulnerability tomorrow.

Chapter 10 – Measuring What Matters Most

Why Measurement Is a Leadership Imperative

The most common mistake in poverty-related work is confusing **activity** with **impact**.
 We proudly report:

- "500 people attended our workshop."
- "10,000 meals distributed."
- "50 new homes built."

These are outputs — important, yes, but they don't tell us if lives have truly changed. Did the workshop participants secure better jobs? Are the families who received meals now food secure? Do the new homes remain affordable five years later?

Leaders who break poverty measure what **lasts**, not just what happens in the moment.

The Risks of Measuring the Wrong Things

- **False Success** – Programs may appear effective on paper while failing in reality.

- **Misaligned Priorities** – Teams chase easy-to-count numbers instead of tackling root causes.
- **Eroded Trust** – Funders and communities lose confidence if results don't match promises.

The fix? Shift from **output-based metrics** to **outcome-based metrics** — from counting what we do to proving what we change.

Three Levels of Measurement for Poverty-Breaking Work

1. **Outputs** – Tangible activities delivered (e.g., number of people trained).
2. **Outcomes** – Medium-term changes in behavior, skills, or conditions (e.g., percentage of trainees who secure stable jobs).
3. **Impact** – Long-term, systemic shifts (e.g., reduction in unemployment rates across the community).

Poverty-breaking leaders track all three — but give highest priority to outcomes and impact.

Case Study 1: The Multidimensional Poverty Index (MPI)

The MPI measures poverty beyond income, including education, health, and living standards. By tracking multiple dimensions, countries like Bhutan and Colombia have been able to target interventions more precisely and measure progress more holistically.

Lesson for Leaders: Broaden your definition of success — poverty is multidimensional, so your measurement must be too.

Case Study 2: Global Health Initiative's Outcome Tracking

A health program in East Africa shifted from counting vaccines administered to tracking reductions in disease incidence over a 5-year period. While outputs stayed steady, outcomes revealed that certain strategies were more effective than others — leading to better allocation of resources.

Lesson for Leaders: Measurement is not just reporting — it's a decision-making tool.

How to Design a Measurement System That Works

Step 1 – Define Success Before You Start

- Ask: "If we succeed, what will be different in people's lives?"
- Make it specific and measurable.

Step 2 – Choose the Right Indicators

- Combine quantitative (e.g., income levels) and qualitative (e.g., self-reported life satisfaction) measures.
- Select a manageable number of metrics so tracking is realistic.

Step 3 – Build Feedback Loops

- Collect data regularly — quarterly or semi-annually — and use it to adjust strategy.

Step 4 – Share Results Transparently

- Report both wins and setbacks; trust grows when you are honest about what's working and what isn't.

From Data Collection to Data Culture

Numbers mean little without a culture that values them. In an **impact culture**:

- Staff see measurements as essential, not as extra paperwork.
- Leaders model data-driven decision-making.
- Communities are involved in defining what success looks like — and in interpreting the results.

The Leadership Mindset for Measuring What Matters

Effective measurement requires humility. You must be willing to discover that a cherished program isn't working as hoped — and then change it. This is where many leaders fail: they protect the program instead of protecting the mission.

Poverty-breaking leaders commit to the mission above any single initiative.

A Challenge to the Reader

Review your current indicators and ask:

- Do they measure *activity* or *lasting change*?

- Are we tracking what matters most to the community, or just what's easiest to count?
- How will we know — beyond numbers — that our work has transformed lives?

Choose one metric this month to refine so it better reflects your true impact.

Chapter 11 – Leveraging Technology Without Losing Humanity

Why Technology Is a Game-Changer — and a Risk

In the fight against poverty, technology can shrink distances, lower costs, and speed up impact. Mobile banking gives the unbanked access to credit. Telemedicine brings healthcare to rural areas. E-learning opens classrooms to millions.

But technology is not a magic bullet. Without careful design, it can **widen inequality** — favoring those who already have access and leaving the most marginalized further behind. It can also strip away the human connection that builds trust and dignity in communities.

The poverty-breaking leader's challenge is to **harness tech as a servant, not a master** — ensuring it accelerates change without dehumanizing the people it aims to help.

The Digital Divide: A Barrier to Inclusion

The "digital divide" isn't just about internet access. It's also about:

- **Affordability** – Devices and data plans still cost more than many can afford.
- **Skills Gap** – People may have smartphones but lack digital literacy.
- **Relevance** – Apps and platforms are often designed without considering local languages, needs, or cultural contexts.

Leaders must bridge this divide before technology can be a true equalizer.

Three Principles for Human-Centered Tech in Poverty Solutions

1. **Design for Inclusion from Day One**
   - Co-create tech solutions with communities to ensure relevance.
   - Support multiple languages and accessibility features.
2. **Pair Technology with Human Support**
   - Combine digital tools with face-to-face guidance, especially in early adoption phases.
   - Example: Digital agricultural platforms that also provide in-person training for farmers.
3. **Measure Human Outcomes, Not Just Tech Adoption**

- Track whether the technology actually improves quality of life — not just how many people download an app or attend an online training.

Case Study 1: Mobile Banking in Sub-Saharan Africa

Platforms like M-Pesa revolutionized access to financial services for millions. By allowing people to send, receive, and store money securely via mobile phones, entire communities were lifted from cash dependency.

The success came not just from the tech, but from **agent networks** — human intermediaries who taught users, built trust, and bridged the gap between the digital and physical.

Lesson for Leaders: Tech adoption is faster and deeper when human support structures are built alongside it.

Case Study 2: Telemedicine in Rural Latin America

A network of clinics introduced telemedicine to connect rural patients with urban specialists. While the technology was sound, adoption was slow until **local health workers** were trained to facilitate consultations, explain diagnoses, and follow up on care plans.

Lesson for Leaders: Technology succeeds when it strengthens — not replaces — human relationships.

Making Technology Work for the Most Marginalized

Step 1 – Start with the Problem, Not the Tool
Don't chase the newest technology because it's trendy. Identify the problem first, then choose the right tool.

Step 2 – Build Capacity Alongside the Solution
Offer training, mentorship, and technical support to ensure the tech is usable by all, especially first-time users.

Step 3 – Ensure Long-Term Access
Plan for maintenance, upgrades, and affordable access so the technology remains functional and relevant over time.

Ethics in Tech-Driven Poverty Work

Poverty-breaking leaders must also navigate ethical concerns:

- **Data Privacy** – Protect sensitive personal information.

- **Bias in AI and Algorithms** – Ensure decision-making tools do not discriminate.
- **Tech Dependency** – Avoid creating systems that communities can't maintain without costly outside help.

The rule is simple: **If it doesn't protect dignity, it's not a solution.**

A Challenge to the Reader

Ask yourself:

- Does my current use of technology include everyone — or only those already connected?
- Am I pairing tech with the human relationships needed for trust and adoption?
- How will I know if the tech is truly improving lives, not just adding features?

Make one adjustment this month to make your tech approach more inclusive, ethical, and human-centered.

Chapter 12 – Resilience in Leadership: Thriving in the Long Fight

Why Resilience Is a Strategic Advantage

Poverty-breaking leadership is not a sprint. It's a marathon with hills, headwinds, and moments where the finish line feels invisible.

The challenges are complex. The timelines are long. The wins can be slow and incremental. Without resilience, leaders risk exhaustion, disillusionment, and burnout — all of which weaken the movement they've worked so hard to build.

Resilience isn't just about surviving; it's about **thriving while leading**, maintaining clarity, creativity, and courage over years, not months.

The Leadership Reality Check

Leaders in this space face unique pressures:

- **Emotional Load** – Constant exposure to hardship can lead to compassion fatigue.
- **Resource Scarcity** – Chronic underfunding demands doing more with less.

- **Public Scrutiny** – Every choice is watched and often criticized.
- **Personal Sacrifice** – Time, family, and personal health often take a backseat.

Resilient leaders recognize these pressures early and build systems to manage them.

Three Dimensions of Resilience

1. **Personal Resilience** – The ability to recover mentally and emotionally from setbacks.
   - Practices: Restorative routines, healthy boundaries, reflection time.
2. **Team Resilience** – The collective capacity to sustain motivation and performance.
   - Practices: Celebrating small wins, rotating responsibilities to avoid burnout, fostering psychological safety.
3. **Organizational Resilience** – Structures and strategies that keep the mission alive in crises.
   - Practices: Diversified funding, contingency planning, succession readiness.

Case Study 1: Disaster Recovery Leadership in the Philippines

In the aftermath of Typhoon Haiyan, local NGO leaders worked around the clock to coordinate relief and rebuilding. Many adopted a **"buddy system"** — pairing leaders to share responsibilities, monitor each other's well-being, and ensure no one carried the emotional load alone.

Lesson for Leaders: Resilience is built in community, not isolation.

Case Study 2: The Long Game in Education Reform

In one South African education initiative, leaders knew change would take decades. They intentionally set **10-year milestones** rather than annual make-or-break targets, allowing the team to see progress without burning out on unrealistic timelines.

Lesson for Leaders: Pacing the work protects both the people and the mission.

Building Your Resilience Toolkit

For Yourself

- **Daily Non-Negotiables:** Sleep, exercise, reflection, or spiritual practice.

- **Boundaries:** Learn to say "no" without guilt when requests don't serve the mission.
- **Mentorship & Peer Support:** Regular check-ins with other leaders who understand the unique challenges.

For Your Team

- Create space for honest conversations about stress and capacity.
- Rotate high-pressure roles and allow recovery time.
- Recognize and celebrate progress frequently.

For Your Organization

- Diversify revenue sources to withstand funding shifts.
- Document critical processes so operations can continue if key people step back.
- Train multiple leaders to step into key roles when needed.

The Mindset Shift from Endurance to Sustainability

Resilience is not about "toughing it out" until you collapse. It's about building a **sustainable rhythm** — knowing when to push hard and when to rest.

Leaders who last in the poverty-breaking arena treat self-care as mission-critical, not self-indulgent. They understand that a burned-out leader cannot inspire, innovate, or sustain impact.

A Challenge to the Reader

- Identify one personal habit that would make you more resilient if practiced consistently.
- Identify one change in your team's culture that could reduce burnout.
- Identify one organizational shift that would make your work less fragile.

Choose one of these to implement in the next 30 days. Resilience grows through small, repeated actions — not sudden overhauls.

Part III – Leader Journeys: Lessons from the Frontlines

Chapter 13 – From Violence to Vitality: The Medellín Transformation

A City at Rock Bottom

In the early 1990s, Medellín, Colombia, was labeled the most dangerous city in the world. Homicide rates were staggering. Drug cartels, led by Pablo Escobar's empire, dominated daily life. Entire neighborhoods were controlled by armed groups. Poverty and inequality were woven into the city's fabric, fueling unrest and hopelessness.

For many cities, the situation might have seemed irreversible. But Medellín's leaders — political, civic, and community-based — refused to accept this as the city's destiny. They imagined something radically different: a Medellín known not for violence, but for innovation, opportunity, and inclusion.

The Vision: Medellín, the Most Innovative City in the World

The transformation began with a bold, clear vision:
"To make Medellín a city of life, learning, and opportunity — a place where every resident can thrive."

This vision wasn't just aspirational. It was **specific, measurable, and shared**. Leaders committed to:

- Reducing violence and crime.
- Expanding education and job opportunities.
- Connecting marginalized communities to the city's economic core.
- Creating public spaces that belonged to everyone.

The vision redefined Medellín's identity. No longer would it be defined by what was broken — it would be defined by what it could become.

From Vision to Action: Integrated Urban Transformation

The city's leaders didn't tackle problems in isolation. They knew crime, poverty, education, and infrastructure were interconnected — and their solutions had to be, too.

Key Actions:

1. **Urban Mobility for Inclusion**
   - Built cable cars (Metrocable) linking hillside neighborhoods — some of the poorest and most isolated — to the metro system and city center.
   - Installed outdoor escalators to make travel easier in steep, hard-to-reach communities.

2. **Education as the Centerpiece**
   - Constructed modern libraries, schools, and learning parks in marginalized areas.
   - Integrated vocational training into community hubs so residents could improve without leaving their neighborhoods.

3. **Public Space as a Crime-Fighting Tool**
   - Designed safe, vibrant public plazas and parks that encouraged community gathering and deterred gang activity.

4. **Public-Private Partnerships**
   - Engaged local businesses to invest in social and infrastructure projects.
   - Leveraged international recognition to attract funding and expertise.

The Impact: Numbers and Narratives

By 2012, Medellín's homicide rate had dropped by over 80% from its peak in the early 1990s. Poverty levels decreased significantly, and the city became a magnet for entrepreneurs, tourists, and global conferences.

In 2013, Medellín was named **"Innovative City of the Year"** by the Urban Land Institute, beating out cities like New York and Tel Aviv.

But the real impact was in the stories:

- Teenagers who once saw gangs as their only future now enrolling in engineering programs.
- Formerly neglected neighborhoods becoming centers of cultural pride.
- Communities taking ownership of public spaces, keeping them clean, safe, and active.

Leadership Lessons from Medellín

1. **Big Problems Require Integrated Solutions**
   - Crime reduction wasn't achieved through policing alone — it came from connecting people to opportunity.
2. **Infrastructure Can Be Social Policy**
   - A cable car wasn't just transport — it was a bridge to jobs, education, and dignity.
3. **Symbols Matter**
   - Building a world-class library in a poor neighborhood sent a message: *You are worth investing in.*
4. **Partnership Multiplies Impact**
   - Government, private sector, and community leaders shared ownership of the change.

Applying the Lessons Globally

Any city or community, regardless of size, can adapt
Medellín's approach:

- Start with a vision bold enough to inspire collective
  action.
- Identify interconnected solutions that address root
  causes, not just symptoms.
- Use infrastructure and public space to promote
  equality and inclusion.
- Engage every sector as an active partner, not a passive
  supporter.

A Challenge to the Reader

Look at your own context — your city, your community,
your organization:

- Where are people physically or socially cut off from
  opportunity?
- What bold, symbolic investments could shift both
  access and mindset?
- Who needs to be at the table to make it happen?

Medellín's story proves that transformation is possible even in the most challenging environments — when leaders choose to see beyond what is and commit to building what could be.

Chapter 14 – Microfinance and Women's Empowerment: The Grameen Story

The Problem No Bank Wanted to Solve

In the 1970s, rural Bangladesh was gripped by deep poverty. Entire communities survived on subsistence farming and small-scale trade. For many women, economic activity meant weaving baskets, making clay pots, or selling produce — but without capital, they were trapped in a cycle of tiny profits and high-interest debt to local moneylenders.

Traditional banks wouldn't touch these borrowers. They were considered "too poor to be creditworthy" — lacking collateral, steady income, or formal credit histories. The system was designed to exclude them.

The Vision: Banking for the Poorest

In 1976, economics professor Muhammad Yunus had a radical idea: **what if the poorest people, especially women, were given small loans with no collateral — and trusted to repay them?**

His vision was grounded in three beliefs:

1. Poverty is not a lack of ability, but a lack of opportunity.
2. Access to credit is a human right.
3. Women, when given economic power, transform not only their own lives but their entire communities.

From Vision to Action: The Grameen Model

1. **Group Lending**
   - Borrowers formed groups of five. While each received their own loan, the group collectively supported and encouraged repayment.
   - This structure-built accountability without legal contracts.

2. **Small, Purposeful Loans**
   - Loans were typically under $100 — enough to buy a sewing machine, purchase raw materials, or start a small trade.
   - Repayments were made weekly, in small, manageable amounts.

3. **No Collateral, No Legal Enforcement**

- Trust, not collateral, was the foundation. Repayment rates averaged over 95%.

4. **Women as the Primary Borrowers**
   - Women made up over 90% of clients, as they were more likely to reinvest earnings in their families' health, nutrition, and education.

The Impact: Beyond Numbers

Since its founding, Grameen Bank has lent billions of dollars to millions of people, primarily women. But the deeper impact has been social:

- Increased school attendance among children of borrowers.
- Improved nutrition and healthcare access.
- Greater decision-making power for women within their households and communities.

Entire villages began shifting from survival mode to growth mode.

Case Study: A Single Loan, A Ripple Effect

A woman named Ayesha used her first Grameen loan to buy a cow. With milk sales, she paid back her loan, bought another cow, and eventually diversified into poultry. Today, her children attend university. Her success inspired other women in her village to join the program — creating a self-reinforcing cycle of empowerment.

Leadership Lessons from Grameen

1. **Challenge the System's Assumptions**
   - Conventional wisdom said the poor couldn't repay loans. Grameen proved otherwise.

2. **Trust as Capital**
   - In contexts where legal enforcement is impractical, social trust can be a more powerful repayment driver.

3. **Empower the Multipliers**
   - Investing in women amplifies impact across families and generations.

4. **Scale Without Losing the Mission**
   - Grameen's principles have been replicated in over 100 countries while maintaining their core focus on dignity and empowerment.

Global Adaptations of the Model

From microfinance programs in Kenya's informal settlements to indigenous-led lending circles in Canada, the Grameen model has inspired localized adaptations that keep the heart of the idea intact while adjusting for cultural and economic realities.

A Challenge to the Reader

Think about your own leadership context:

- What "unbanked" or excluded groups exist in your community?

- How could you design a trust-based access system for them — whether in finance, education, or opportunity?

- Who are the "multipliers" you could empower for the greatest ripple effect?

The Grameen story proves that when leaders challenge outdated assumptions and invest in the people everyone else overlooks, they can spark movements that reshape entire economies

Chapter 15 – Education as a Gateway: Pratham's India Model

The Problem: School Attendance Without Learning

In the early 1990s, India had made major strides in getting children into school. But a harsh truth emerged: **attendance did not equal education**.

Nationwide surveys showed that millions of children in Grade 5 could not read a simple Grade 2 text or do basic arithmetic. The system was producing students with years of schooling but without the skills needed to progress, work, or fully participate in society.

For children from low-income families, this learning gap meant that even with a school uniform and a seat in class, their futures were still blocked.

The Vision: Every Child in School — and Learning Well

Pratham, founded in 1995, started with a clear, disruptive vision:

"Learning for all, not just schooling for all."

The goal was not simply to increase enrollment, but to ensure every child mastered foundational reading and math skills — the gateways to all other learning.

From Vision to Action: The Pratham Approach

1. **Teaching at the Right Level (TaRL)**
   - Children were grouped by learning level, not age or grade.
   - Instruction focused on building foundational skills before moving to advanced content.

2. **Community Volunteers as Educators**
   - Pratham recruited and trained local volunteers, often young women from the same community, to teach in short-term learning camps.
   - This expanded reach at low cost and strengthened community ownership.

3. **Annual Status of Education Report (ASER)**
   - Pratham developed the ASER survey to assess basic learning across rural India.

- The report became a national benchmark, influencing government policy and funding priorities.

4. **Low-Cost, High-Impact Materials**

- Simple reading cards, locally relevant stories, and practical math tools replaced expensive, complex textbooks for early learners.

The Impact: Scaling Simplicity

Over two decades, Pratham has reached tens of millions of children across India and other countries. Independent evaluations show that **TaRL significantly improves literacy and numeracy within months**.

More importantly, the approach has been adopted by multiple state governments, embedding the model into public education systems and extending its reach to millions more.

Case Study: The Village Learning Camp

In one rural village in Uttar Pradesh, only 3 of 30 Grade 4 students could read a simple story. After a 40-day Pratham learning camp, 22 of them could. Parents, once skeptical, began advocating for the methods to be used in the regular school system.

Leadership Lessons from Pratham

1. **Redefine the Goal**

   - Enrollment is not enough. Define success by outcomes that matter for life, not just for statistics.

2. **Keep It Simple to Scale It Fast**
   - The TaRL model uses minimal resources, making it easy to replicate and adapt.

3. **Measure Publicly, Act Transparently**
   - The ASER report's open data kept pressure on governments to respond and improve.

4. **Mobilize Local Talent**
   - Community volunteers not only filled teaching gaps but became role models for the children they taught.

Global Relevance

Pratham's approach has been adapted in countries from
Ghana to Mexico, proving that the principle of "teaching at
the right level" works wherever children are falling behind.

A Challenge to the Reader

Ask yourself:

- In my field, what is the equivalent of "attendance
  without learning"?
- Am I measuring the real outcomes, or just the visible
  inputs?
- How could I simplify my solution so it can scale
  quickly without losing quality?

Pratham's story shows that the simplest, most targeted
interventions can often deliver the most profound
transformations — if leaders are willing to focus relentlessly
on what truly matters.

Chapter 16 – Rebuilding Rwanda: Vision 2020 in Action

From National Trauma to National Determination

In 1994, Rwanda experienced one of the worst tragedies of the 20th century — the genocide against the Tutsi, in which over 800,000 people were killed in just 100 days. The country was left shattered: infrastructure destroyed, institutions broken, and a society deeply traumatized.

Many nations facing such devastation might have resigned themselves to decades of stagnation and instability. Rwanda's leadership chose a different path — one of unity, resilience, and an unrelenting focus on development.

The Vision: Middle-Income Status Within a Generation

Launched in 2000, **Vision 2020** aimed to transform Rwanda from a low-income, agriculture-dependent country into a knowledge-based, middle-income economy by the year 2020.

The vision had six key pillars:

1. **Good Governance** – Eradicating corruption and building accountable institutions.

2. **Human Resource Development** – Expanding education and health services.

3. **Private Sector Growth** – Creating an environment for entrepreneurship and investment.

4. **Infrastructure Development** – Roads, energy, ICT, and urban planning.

5. **Productive Agriculture** – Increasing yields and connecting farmers to markets.

6. **Regional and International Integration** – Opening Rwanda to global trade and partnerships.

From Vision to Action: The Strategic Blueprint

1. **Governance Reform**
    o   Anti-corruption measures and performance contracts ("Imihigo") for public officials.
    o   Decentralized government to empower local decision-making.

2. **Education Overhaul**
    o   Free primary education and expanded secondary schooling.
    o   Curriculum shifts toward science, technology, and entrepreneurship.

3. **Healthcare Expansion**
   - Community-based health insurance covering over 90% of the population.
   - Significant reductions in maternal and child mortality.

4. **Economic Diversification**
   - Investment in tourism, ICT, and services alongside agriculture.
   - Kigali developed into a regional conference and business hub.

5. **Infrastructure Investment**
   - Paved roads, expanded electricity access, and a national fiber-optic network.

The Impact: Numbers and Narratives

- Poverty rate fell from 77% in 1994 to 55% by 2017.
- GDP growth averaged 7–8% annually for two decades.
- Life expectancy more than doubled from the mid-1990s to over 69 years.
- Rwanda became one of the least corrupt countries in Africa, according to Transparency International.

Beyond statistics, the country cultivated a renewed sense of national identity — shifting from ethnic division toward a shared Rwandan identity.

Case Study: The Coffee Sector Revival

By focusing on quality over quantity, Rwanda's coffee farmers moved from selling low-grade beans to producing premium coffee for international markets. This shift raised incomes for thousands of rural families and positioned Rwanda as a respected brand in global specialty coffee.

Leadership Lessons from Vision 2020

1. **Clarity of Vision Anchors the Nation**
   - A shared, time-bound vision provided alignment across all sectors.
2. **Accountability Drives Performance**
   - Public officials' performance contracts tied personal credibility to national progress.
3. **Invest in People First**
   - Health and education were prioritized as the foundation for all other growth.
4. **Global Partnerships Multiply Impact**
   - Rwanda actively sought foreign investment and knowledge exchange while ensuring local ownership of initiatives.

Adapting the Lessons

While Rwanda's context is unique, its approach holds lessons for any leader:

- Align every initiative with a unified, measurable vision.
- Make accountability a daily practice, not an annual review.
- Focus on human capital as the driver of long-term prosperity.

A Challenge to the Reader

In your sphere of influence — whether a city, organization, or community — ask:

- What is our equivalent of "Vision 2020"?
- How do we hold ourselves accountable for progress?
- Are we building our strategy on the foundation of human potential?

Rwanda's story proves that even from the deepest devastation, a clear vision, disciplined action, and united leadership can create a thriving future.

Chapter 17 – Local Innovation, Global Reach: The Kenya Clean Water Coalition

The Problem: Water Scarcity Beyond Infrastructure

In many rural parts of Kenya, the challenge of clean water wasn't simply the absence of wells or filtration systems — it was **the breakdown of existing solutions**.
 Wells fell into disrepair because spare parts were unavailable or too costly. Filtration units sat unused because no one had been trained to maintain them. Aid projects came and went, leaving behind hardware without long-term ownership.

For families — often women and children — this meant walking hours each day to collect water, limiting time for school, work, or community activities.

The Vision: Reliable, Locally Managed Water for Every Household

A group of Kenyan NGOs, engineering firms, community leaders, and government agencies formed the **Kenya Clean Water Coalition** with a shared goal:
 "Every household in target communities will have

sustainable access to safe, affordable water, managed by the people who use it."

This vision recognized that water access is not just an infrastructure issue — it's a **governance and capacity issue**.

From Vision to Action: Building a Sustainable Water System

1. **Co-Design with Communities**
   - Local leaders were involved from the outset, identifying water points, governance structures, and payment models that fit community norms.

2. **Technical Excellence Meets Local Skills**
   - Engineering firms provided robust designs using durable, locally available materials.
   - Community members were trained as technicians to handle repairs, ensuring systems didn't collapse when outside experts left.

3. **Micro-Payment Systems**
   - Households contributed a small monthly fee for water use, creating a maintenance fund.
   - Mobile payment platforms made fee collection transparent and accountable.

4. **Partnership Accountability**
   - NGOs monitored water quality and usage.

- Local committees publicly reported on finances and maintenance schedules.

The Impact: From Fetching to Flowing

- Average daily water collection time dropped from 3–4 hours to under 30 minutes.
- Incidence of waterborne diseases fell by more than 60% in participating villages.
- Women reported having more time for income-generating activities; children had more consistent school attendance.

Perhaps most tellingly, 95% of systems installed under the Coalition's model were still operational after five years — a striking improvement over previous interventions.

Case Study: The Village of Makueni

Before the Coalition's intervention, the nearest clean water source was a two-hour walk away. By involving the village council in the design, training local youth as water technicians, and setting a community-managed fee structure, Makueni not only sustained its system but expanded it to serve neighboring settlements.

Leadership Lessons from the Coalition

1. **Sustainability Requires Local Ownership**
   - Communities must control the system — from decision-making to daily maintenance.

2. **Partnership Is the Engine**
   - Government, NGOs, business, and citizens each played essential, complementary roles.

3. **Small Payments, Big Results**
   - Affordable micro-payments created dignity, accountability, and a sense of shared investment.

4. **Capacity Is as Important as Capital**
   - Infrastructure without training is just expensive scrap metal.

Global Applications

This approach can be adapted to other essential services — electricity, sanitation, internet access — wherever long-term sustainability is a challenge. The key is pairing **technical innovation with community capacity** and **shared accountability**.

A Challenge to the Reader

Think about the "clean water" equivalent in your context — the essential resource or service that fails because it lacks ownership, maintenance, or local capacity.

- How could you bring multiple sectors together to address it?
- What training or governance structures would ensure it lasts?
- How could you embed accountability, so it doesn't depend on you or your organization alone?

The Kenya Clean Water Coalition proves that when solutions are **co-owned, co-created, and co-managed**, they last — and they spread.

Chapter 18 – From Informal Settlements to Economic Hubs: The Brazil Co-op Movement

The Problem: Work Without Security

Brazil's sprawling urban favelas are home to millions. They are vibrant, creative communities — but historically, they've been excluded from formal economic systems. Many residents survive through informal, low-wage work with no contracts, benefits, or job security.

The result was a cycle of **underemployment**: people working long hours for survival wages, unable to save, invest, or build long-term stability. The economic potential of these communities was vast — but untapped.

The Vision: Economic Dignity Through Self-Owned Enterprises

In the early 2000s, a group of favela leaders, NGOs, and local universities envisioned a different future:

"Transform favelas into economic hubs where residents control their own businesses, profits, and future."

They believed that cooperatives — collectively owned and democratically managed enterprises — could formalize work, increase incomes, and strengthen community governance.

From Vision to Action: Building the Co-op Network

1. **Skills Mapping and Training**
   - Community workshops identified existing skills — from carpentry to catering — and offered business and financial literacy training.

2. **Legal and Institutional Support**
   - Universities provided legal assistance to formally register cooperatives.
   - NGOs offered governance training so members could manage operations democratically.

3. **Shared Infrastructure**
   - Co-ops pooled resources to purchase equipment, rent workspace, and market their services collectively.

4. **Market Linkages**

- Partnerships with businesses and municipal governments opened contracts for cleaning, catering, construction, and manufacturing.

The Impact: Ownership Changes Everything

- **Income Gains** – Co-op members often doubled or tripled their earnings compared to previous informal work.
- **Stability** – Formal contracts and pooled savings provided a safety net during slow seasons.
- **Community Investment** – Profits were reinvested into local schools, health clinics, and youth programs.
- **Empowerment** – Members gained leadership skills and a stronger voice in local decision-making.

Case Study: The Women's Catering Cooperative in Rio

A group of women who had been working as domestic helpers formed a catering co-op, pooling their cooking skills and kitchen equipment. Within two years, they secured contracts to cater corporate events and municipal functions. Their success inspired other women to start co-ops in tailoring, cleaning, and event planning — creating a local network of women-led businesses.

Leadership Lessons from the Co-op Movement

1. **Ownership Fuels Commitment**
   - People work differently when they have a direct stake in the outcome.

2. **Leverage Existing Skills**
   - Start with what the community already knows how to do well.

3. **Partnerships Open Markets**
   - External allies can connect co-ops to larger clients and contracts.

4. **Democracy Builds Capacity**
   - Shared decision-making strengthens both the enterprise and the community.

Global Potential

The co-op model is not unique to Brazil. Similar movements have taken root in South Africa's townships, Italy's Emilia-Romagna region, and worker-owned businesses in the United States. Wherever people face systemic exclusion from formal markets, cooperatives can be a bridge to ownership and stability.

A Challenge to the Reader

Ask yourself:

- Where in my community are people locked out of economic opportunity?
- Could collective ownership create stability and scale for them?
- Who could partner to provide the legal, financial, or market access they'd need?

The Brazil Co-op Movement shows that when communities take control of their economic destiny, they don't just lift incomes — they lift aspirations, confidence, and the entire local economy.

Closing Part III – Leadership Beyond Borders

Across Medellín, Bangladesh, India, Rwanda, Kenya, and Brazil, the through-line is clear:

- **Vision** rooted in hope and specificity.
- **Action** that is integrated, inclusive, and context-aware.
- **Impact** that changes systems, not just circumstances.

These leaders — whether city mayors, grassroots organizers, national policymakers, or community entrepreneurs — prove that poverty is not inevitable. The next step is for you, the reader, to take these lessons and translate them into your own leadership context.

Part IV – Your Leadership Roadmap

Chapter 19 – Define Your Leadership Arena

Why Your Starting Point Matters

Leaders often fail to create lasting change because they start too broadly or in areas where they lack real influence. They take on *everything* and end up moving nothing.

The first step in your poverty-breaking roadmap is to identify your **leadership arena** — the place where your skills, resources, and network intersect with a community's most urgent needs. This is where you can have the greatest leverage and credibility.

Your arena might be:

- A **sector** (education, healthcare, housing, small business, agriculture).
- A **community** (a neighborhood, rural district, or specific demographic group).
- A **system** (supply chains, workforce pipelines, financial access, policy reform).

Choosing your arena isn't about limiting your vision — it's about focusing your first phase so you can prove results and build momentum.

The Three Filters for Choosing Your Arena

1. **Where You Have Influence**
   - Influence comes from position, relationships, expertise, or reputation.
   - Ask: "Where would my calls get answered? Where would my ideas be heard?"

2. **Where the Need Is Clear and Significant**
   - Look for areas where poverty's impact is visible and measurable.
   - Ask: "Where is there urgency? Where will solving one problem unlock others?"

3. **Where There's a Path to Early Wins**
   - Starting with achievable wins builds trust and attracts allies.
   - Ask: "What can we realistically improve in the next 6–12 months?"

Case Example: A CEO's Arena

A manufacturing CEO wanted to address poverty in her city. She had deep influence with local employers, but no direct experience in education or housing. Her arena became **workforce development** — building a coalition of companies to create apprenticeship programs for unemployed youth. She leveraged her relationships for quick wins, then expanded into related issues like housing for workers.

Step 1 – Map Your Sphere of Influence

Draw three circles:

- **People** – Who do you have direct access to? (colleagues, partners, policymakers, community leaders)
- **Places** – Which communities, organizations, or sectors do you know well?
- **Platforms** – Where can you get your message heard? (media, events, social networks)

The overlap is your influence zone.

Step 2 – Map Needs and Assets

List the community's most pressing poverty-related challenges. Then list existing strengths or resources in that same space. The sweet spot is where urgent need meets available assets you can mobilize.

Step 3 – Choose Your Entry Point

Your entry point should be small enough to act on quickly, but significant enough to matter.

 Examples:

- Improving school attendance for girls in one district.
- Creating micro-loan access for street vendors in a single neighborhood.
- Reducing transportation barriers for rural job seekers.

Avoid the "Everywhere at Once" Trap

Your arena is the launchpad, not the whole rocket. Once you've proven results, you can expand — but starting everywhere spreads resources thin and makes success harder to measure.

A Challenge to the Reader

Complete these prompts:

1. My greatest current influence is in

   _____.

2. The poverty-related need I see most clearly is

   _____.

3. A realistic first win in the next 6–12 months could be

    _____.

These answers will define your leadership arena — the foundation for everything you'll build in the chapters ahead.

Chapter 20 – Craft Your Vision Statement

Why Vision Is Your Leadership North Star

Once you know your leadership arena, the next step is to define **what you are aiming for**. Without a vision, you risk drifting into disconnected activities, reacting to every opportunity or challenge without a clear direction.

Your vision is not a slogan. It's a **picture of a preferred future** that is bold enough to inspire others, specific enough to guide decisions, and measurable enough to track progress.

A strong vision answers the question:

> *"If we succeed, what will be different — and for whom?"*

The Three Qualities of a Poverty-Breaking Vision

1. **Clarity** – Everyone who hears it understands the end goal.
2. **Boldness** – It challenges the status quo and stretches what people think is possible.

3. **Credibility** – It's ambitious but achievable, grounded in your arena's realities.

Vision vs. Mission vs. Goals

- **Vision:** *Where you're going.* (destination)
- **Mission:** *Why you exist.* (purpose)
- **Goals:** *The steps you'll take to get there.* (milestones)

Example:

- Vision: *Every household in the district has access to affordable, safe drinking water.*
- Mission: *To mobilize communities and partners to build and maintain sustainable water systems.*
- Goal: *Install 50 community-managed water points in the next two years.*

Case Study: Medellín's Vision

In Chapter 13, we saw how Medellín's leaders rallied the city around the idea of becoming "the most innovative city in the world." That vision guided every infrastructure project, education reform, and community investment for over a decade. It was clear, bold, and big enough to require — and inspire — collaboration.

Crafting Your Vision: A Step-by-Step Process

Step 1 – Start with the "Who"

Who will benefit from your work? Be specific — "families in rural Ward 7," "women entrepreneurs under 30," "school-aged children in urban neighborhoods."

Step 2 – Define the Change

What will be different in their lives because of your leadership? Focus on outcomes, not just activities.

Step 3 – Set a Time Horizon

Choose a realistic but motivating time frame — often 3–10 years for systemic change.

Step 4 – Test for the Three Qualities

Ask: Is it clear? Is it bold? Is it credible?

Vision Statement Examples

- *By 2030, every unemployed youth in our city will have access to training, mentorship, and a pathway to a living-wage job.*
- *Within five years, all street vendors in our district will operate under fair, formalized contracts with access to microfinance and health benefits.*

- *Every rural school in our region will have reliable internet access and trained digital literacy instructors by 2027.*

Common Vision Pitfalls to Avoid

- **Too Vague:** "Make life better for the poor" is not actionable.
- **Too Small:** Goals disguised as visions don't inspire broad support.
- **Too Unrealistic:** A vision that's obviously impossible will erode trust.

A Challenge to the Reader

Complete this sentence using your leadership arena from Chapter 19:

> *By (year), (specific group) will (specific change) because of (your initiative).*

Refine it until it is clear, bold, and credible. This is your **leadership vision** — the North Star that will guide every decision, partnership, and action in your roadmap.

Chapter 21 – Build Your First-Phase Action Plan

Why a Vision Without a Plan Fails

A strong vision can inspire, but without a plan it will drift into wishful thinking. The first-phase action plan is your **bridge between vision and impact** — a focused, time-bound roadmap that makes progress visible and momentum sustainable.

This phase is not about doing everything at once. It's about identifying **the right early moves** that will:

- Prove your approach works.
- Build credibility with stakeholders.
- Attract the resources and partners you'll need for scale.

The 3 Elements of a First-Phase Plan

1. **High-Leverage Actions**
   - Focus on actions that remove the biggest barriers or unlock the most opportunities in your arena.

- Ask: "If I could only do three things in the next 12 months, which would make the biggest difference?"

2. **Strategic Partners**
   - Identify who must be involved for success.
   - Look for partners with complementary strengths — skills, networks, resources — rather than those who simply agree with you.

3. **Clear Milestones**
   - Break your vision into measurable, achievable targets for the next 90 days, 6 months, and 1 year.
   - This keeps progress visible and helps you course-correct quickly.

Case Study: First-Year Wins in a Youth Employment Initiative

A community leader with a vision to reduce youth unemployment in her city set three first-phase actions:

1. Launch a pilot training program for 50 youth in partnership with two local companies.

2. Secure funding for year two through a blended finance model.

3. Create a public awareness campaign to shift perceptions about hiring youth from disadvantaged backgrounds.

By the end of year one, 38 participants were employed, two more companies joined the coalition, and the program gained national media coverage — setting the stage for expansion.

Step-by-Step: Building Your Plan

Step 1 – Revisit Your Vision Statement
Ensure every action in your plan moves directly toward your stated vision.

Step 2 – Select Your First 3–5 Actions
These should be achievable within 12 months and highly visible in their impact.

Step 3 – Define Who Does What
Clarify roles and responsibilities for your team and partners.

Step 4 – Set Milestones and Deadlines
Map out what success looks like at 90 days, 6 months, and 1 year.

Step 5 – Identify Success Indicators

Choose how you'll measure progress — not just activity — during this phase.

Pro Tips for Early-Phase Leadership

- **Start with the achievable, not the easy.** Early wins should be meaningful enough to inspire confidence, even if they require effort.
- **Communicate often.** Keep stakeholders updated to maintain trust and engagement.
- **Document everything.** Your first-phase journey will be a powerful tool for fundraising, partnership building, and scaling.

A Challenge to the Reader

Take your vision from Chapter 20 and outline:

1. Your top three high-leverage actions.
2. The partners you'll approach in the next 30 days.
3. Your 90-day, 6-month, and 1-year milestones.

Once written, share your plan with at least one trusted peer or mentor for feedback — then start moving.

Chapter 22 – Mobilize Your Allies

Why Allies Multiply Your Impact

Even the most talented, committed leaders will fail if they try to tackle poverty alone. Poverty is complex and interconnected — it demands **cross-sector, multi-skill teams** that can bring different forms of capital: social, financial, intellectual, and political.

Mobilizing allies isn't just about asking for help. It's about creating **shared ownership** of the vision, so others are as invested in the outcome as you are.

The 3 Types of Allies You Need

1. **Strategic Partners**
   - Organizations or individuals whose resources, expertise, or influence directly advance your goals.
   - Examples: local government agencies, businesses, universities, NGOs.

2. **Community Champions**

- Trusted, respected voices inside the
     community you aim to serve.

   - They bring legitimacy, cultural insight, and the
     ability to mobilize local participation.

3. **Amplifiers**
   - People or platforms that can share your vision
     widely, build public support, and attract new
     allies.
   - Examples: journalists, social media
     influencers, faith leaders.

Case Study: The Clean Water Coalition's Ally Map

From Chapter 17, the Kenya Clean Water Coalition didn't
just rely on NGOs. They recruited:

- Local chiefs as **community champions**.
- Engineering firms as **strategic partners**.
- Radio hosts and local journalists as **amplifiers**.

Each played a specific role — and because the vision was
shared from the start, all felt ownership of the results.

Step-by-Step: Mobilizing Your Allies

Step 1 – Map Your Stakeholders

List everyone connected to your arena: potential funders, implementers, beneficiaries, influencers.

Step 2 – Identify Overlap in Interests

Ask: *What do they care about that aligns with my vision?* The best allies see mutual benefit, not charity.

Step 3 – Make a Clear Ask

Be specific: Do you want funding, volunteers, advocacy, or access to their networks?

Step 4 – Build Trust Before You Need It

Engage with potential allies now, not only when you need something urgently.

Step 5 – Formalize the Relationship

Partnership agreements, MOUs, or even informal commitments help ensure accountability and clarity.

Tips for Keeping Allies Engaged

- **Celebrate together.** Publicly acknowledge their contributions in reports, media, and events.
- **Share progress updates.** Transparency builds trust.

- **Create roles that matter.** Give allies meaningful responsibility, not token gestures.

A Challenge to the Reader

From your action plan in Chapter 21:

1. Identify 3–5 potential allies (at least one from each category).
2. Write down what they would gain from joining your initiative.
3. Plan your first outreach — email, call, or in-person meeting — within the next 14 days.

Chapter 23 – Secure Sustainable Resources

Why Sustainability Beats Survival

Many promising poverty-breaking initiatives fail not because the idea was flawed, but because the resources ran out. A one-time grant or a burst of donations can launch a project, but without a plan for **consistent, diversified revenue and material support**, leaders spend more time chasing funds than delivering results.

Sustainable resources free you to focus on **impact**, not just survival.

The 4 Resource Streams Every Leader Should Consider

1. **Financial Capital**
   - Grants, impact investments, earned income, blended finance.
   - Aim for a **mix** so you're not dependent on a single source.
2. **Human Capital**
   - Volunteers, skilled professionals, mentors, trainers.

- Often overlooked, but can be as valuable as cash.

3. **Social Capital**
   - Networks, relationships, endorsements.
   - Opens doors to funders, markets, and policy influence.

4. **Physical Capital**
   - Facilities, equipment, technology, transportation.
   - Shared or donated assets can reduce start-up costs significantly.

Case Study: Financing a Rural Skills Hub

A social entrepreneur in East Africa wanted to open a vocational training center. Instead of relying on donor funding alone, she:

- Partnered with local businesses for tool and equipment donations (**physical capital**).
- Secured a small grant for initial operations (**financial capital**).
- Recruited volunteer instructors from the national technical college (**human capital**).

- Leveraged the mayor's endorsement to gain media coverage and credibility (**social capital**).

This mix allowed her to run the center for two years before needing major new funding.

Step-by-Step: Building Your Sustainable Resource Plan

Step 1 – Identify What You Truly Need
Break your needs into categories: people, money, equipment, networks.

Step 2 – Match Needs to Potential Sources
For each need, list at least three possible sources — local, national, and international.

Step 3 – Diversify Early
Don't wait for one source to say no before seeking others. Multiple streams reduce vulnerability.

Step 4 – Build Long-Term Partnerships
Recurring support agreements are more valuable than one-time gifts.

Step 5 – Track and Report Value
Show partners the impact of their contribution so they'll stay invested.

Overcoming Common Funding Fears

- **Fear of Asking:** Frame it as an investment in shared outcomes, not a personal favor.
- **Fear of Profit in Social Work:** Mission-aligned revenue streams make you more resilient, not less ethical.
- **Fear of Rejection:** Every "no" is information you can use to refine your pitch.

A Challenge to the Reader

From your action plan in Chapter 21:

1. List your top 5 resource needs for the next year.
2. Identify at least 2 potential sources for each.
3. Commit to making your first 3 funding or resource requests within the next 30 days.

Chapter 24 – Measure, Adapt, and Scale

Why Tracking and Adapting Are Non-Negotiable

Resources alone don't guarantee success — **feedback and flexibility** do. Too many initiatives fail because leaders stick to the original plan even when evidence shows it's not working, or they scale prematurely without proof of impact.

The poverty-breaking leader's mantra should be:

> **Measure honestly. Adapt quickly. Scale wisely.**

The Three-Part Cycle of Continuous Improvement

1. **Measure What Matters**
   - Focus on **outcomes**, not just outputs.
   - Example: Don't just track the number of people trained; track how many gained sustainable employment or started profitable businesses.

2. **Adapt in Real Time**
    - ○ Use data to make mid-course corrections.

    - ○ Involve beneficiaries in interpreting results —
      they often spot patterns you'll miss.

3. **Scale with Readiness, Not Just Ambition**
    - ○ Only expand when your model is stable,
      replicable, and resourced for growth.

Case Study: Scaling a Digital Literacy Program

A nonprofit in Southeast Asia started with a pilot serving 200
women. They tracked both digital skills gained and the
women's increased income over six months. When early data
showed that income growth was strongest in rural hubs with
strong community mentors, they adapted the model to focus
on those areas.

When they scaled to 2,000 participants, they carried over the
mentorship component — and saw consistent results.

Lesson: Measure, adapt, then scale.

Step-by-Step: Your Measure–Adapt–Scale Process

Step 1 – Define Success Indicators

Ask: "What change would prove we are achieving our vision?" Choose 3–5 core metrics.

Step 2 – Gather Data Regularly

Quarterly is often enough for big-picture trends, monthly for operational tracking.

Step 3 – Hold Review Meetings

Bring your team and key partners together to discuss findings and decide on changes.

Step 4 – Test Before Expanding

Run small pilots in new locations or sectors before rolling out full-scale.

Step 5 – Secure Resources for Scale

Growth requires increased capacity — staffing, systems, funding — to maintain quality.

Scaling Pitfalls to Avoid

- **Scaling Too Fast:** Expansion without proof of model stability drains resources.

- **Scaling Without Context:** What works in one place may fail elsewhere if you ignore local differences.
- **Scaling Without Leadership Depth:** New locations need empowered leaders, not just brand presence.

A Challenge to the Reader

From your current plan:

1. Identify three outcome-based metrics you'll track over the next year.
2. Commit to one quarterly review where you decide on at least one adaptation.
3. Define the conditions you must meet before scaling (e.g., 80% of participants reaching target outcomes).

Scaling is not about being bigger — it's about being better, in more places, for more people.

Chapter 25 – Lead for the Long Game

Why the Long Game Matters

Poverty-breaking leadership is rarely a quick win. Real change often takes years — sometimes decades — to solidify. Without planning for the long term, even the most promising initiatives risk collapsing when the leader steps back or resources shift.

Your role is not just to drive results **now**, but to ensure those results survive and grow **after you**.

The Three Foundations of Long-Term Leadership

1. **Personal Sustainability**
   - Protect your energy through rest, boundaries, and renewal practices.
   - Remember: you can't lead well for 10 + years if you burn out in year three.

2. **Succession Planning**
   - Identify potential leaders early and give them real responsibility.

- Build leadership teams instead of single points of dependency.

3. **System Embedding**
   - Ensure processes, knowledge, and partnerships are documented and accessible.
   - Integrate your initiative into existing institutions so it's not reliant on you personally.

Case Study: A Housing Nonprofit's Smooth Transition

A housing nonprofit in Latin America avoided collapse when its founder retired by preparing a **three-year succession plan**.

- Two deputy directors were mentored and gradually took over strategic roles.
- Partnerships and funding agreements were renewed in the organization's name, not the founder's.
- A clear operations manual ensured continuity.

The transition was so smooth that donors increased support, seeing the organization's resilience.

Building Resilience Into Your Leadership

Step 1 – Pace Yourself

Design work rhythms that balance urgency with longevity. Build in recovery periods.

Step 2 – Distribute Power

Avoid the "founder's trap" where everything flows through one person. Let others lead projects, manage budgets, and represent the organization externally.

Step 3 – Document and Share

Write down processes, contacts, and lessons learned so successors don't start from zero.

Step 4 – Build a Leadership Pipeline

Invest in training, mentorship, and growth opportunities for emerging leaders.

Leaving a Legacy That Lasts

Your ultimate leadership success is measured not by how essential you are, but by how unnecessary you become — because the mission is bigger than you and able to stand on its own.

The legacy test:

- Will this work keep advancing without me?
- Will it continue to serve its purpose in 5, 10, 20 years?
- Have I created a culture where new ideas and leaders can thrive?

A Challenge to the Reader

Write down:

1. The three biggest risks to your initiative if you stepped away tomorrow.
2. One action you can take in the next 90 days to reduce each risk.
3. The name of at least one emerging leader you can start mentoring now.

The long game isn't about you staying forever — it's about the work staying strong forever.

Part IV – Your Leadership Roadmap

You now have:

- A defined **arena** where you can lead most effectively.
- A **vision** to guide your work.
- A **first-phase action plan** to get started.

- Strategies for mobilizing allies and securing sustainable resources.
- Systems to measure, adapt, and scale.
- Practices to protect your energy and pass the torch.

With this roadmap, you are equipped not just to start strong — but to lead for impact that lasts.

The Poverty-Breaking Leader's Oath

Why This Oath Matters

Every change begins with a choice.

The choice to lead differently.

The choice to believe that poverty — no matter how deep, how persistent, how systemic — can be broken.

The choice to act with courage when the path is unclear, to persist when progress is slow, and to lift others even when your own load feels heavy.

This oath is more than words. It is your declaration — to yourself, to your community, and to the world — that you will not stand on the sidelines while cycles of poverty continue.

It is a personal covenant to lead with vision, act with integrity, and measure success not by what you accumulate, but by what you help others achieve.

The Oath

I pledge to lead as a poverty-breaking leader.
I will see possibilities where others see
permanence.
 I will act with courage where others choose
comfort.
 I will build coalitions that unite across divides,
 And create solutions that outlast my tenure.

I will measure my impact not by how many I
serve today,
 But by how many no longer need my service
tomorrow.

I will invest in people as partners,
 Not as passive recipients of aid.

I will protect my integrity,
 Share my knowledge,
 And raise new leaders who will carry the
mission forward.

I will refuse to accept poverty as inevitable.
 I will work until opportunity is the inheritance
of every child,
 And dignity is the shared right of every adult.

I will lead not only for my time,

But for generations yet to come.

Your Signature

Signed: _____

Date: _____

Keep a copy of this oath where you can see it often — in your office, your journal, or your phone's home screen. Let it remind you that leadership is not a moment; it's a commitment.

Final Words

You are now equipped with the framework, tools, and global examples to break cycles of poverty in your business, community, or nation. But the real work starts beyond these pages — in the conversations you initiate, the partnerships you forge, and the risks you take.

Poverty may be persistent, but so is your capacity to lead change.

Lead with vision.

Act with courage.

Measure with integrity.

And never, ever stop.

Looking Ahead

With this chapter, we close the core framework of **Vision to Action to Impact**. In the **Epilogue**, we will return to the heart of this journey: why this work matters, how far we've come, and what it will take for all of us to lead the change from poverty to prosperity.

Epilogue – From Vision to Impact: A Final Call to Lead Boldly

The Journey Revisited

This book began with a simple but urgent conviction: poverty, though persistent, is not permanent. We have walked through pathways of skill-building, education, workforce readiness, health, parental empowerment, community building, advocacy, wealth creation, and leadership development. We have seen how these strategies, when combined, create a tapestry strong enough to resist the weight of generational poverty.

But strategies alone are not enough. Leadership is the thread that weaves them together. Without leaders who can see boldly, act courageously, and measure faithfully, poverty remains managed rather than broken.

Why Leaders Must Act Now

The global context makes this work more urgent than ever.

- **700 million people** still live in extreme poverty on

less than $2.15 a day (World Bank).

- Climate change threatens to push an additional **130 million people** into poverty by 2030 (UNDP).
- And yet, when leaders align across sectors and borders, we see transformative success stories—from Rwanda's health reforms to Brazil's community empowerment programs, from Singapore's workforce training to Vietnam's poverty index.

These examples prove the point: **the tools exist. What we need is leadership with the courage to use them.**

Vision → Action → Impact: The Leadership Blueprint

As leaders, our mandate is simple but profound:

- **Vision** – to see a future where poverty is not destiny.
- **Action** – to design and execute strategies that bring that vision into reality.
- **Impact** – to measure success by lasting transformation, not temporary relief.

This cycle is not just a framework. It is a **leadership imperative** for anyone who claims the title of leader—

whether of a company, a classroom, a congregation, a city, or a nation.

A Call to Bold Leadership

The leaders history remembers are those who refused to accept inevitability. They saw possibilities others missed. They built coalitions across divides. They measured not by the applause of the present but by the legacy they left for the future.

Now, the same call rests on you.

- Will you collaborate beyond your comfort zone?
- Will you measure outcomes instead of activities?
- Will you build systems that last beyond your tenure?

The Final Word

From Poverty to Prosperity is not just a book—it is an invitation. An invitation to turn **vision into action, and action into impact.**

The next chapter of this story will not be written by me alone. It will be written by leaders like you—leaders who believe that poverty can be broken, prosperity can be shared, and legacy can be measured not by titles or profits, but by lives transformed.

The time is now. The work is global. The responsibility is ours.

Lead boldly. Act decisively. Measure relentlessly. And never forget—poverty is not permanent.

DTD's Leadership Playbook & Blueprint

Introducing DTD's Leadership Playbook & Blueprint

Behind every movement that endures lies a clear playbook—a set of guiding principles that leaders can adapt, apply, and replicate across contexts. For me, that playbook was born out of years of observing what works in communities, businesses, schools, and governments when it comes to breaking the cycle of poverty.

The **Leadership Playbook & Blueprint** is not about abstract theory; it is about **tested practices and transferable strategies** that any leader—whether established or aspiring—can use to transform their sphere of influence. It serves as the connective tissue between the fourteen pathways identified in my earlier works and the integrated framework of *Vision → Action → Impact* that this book presents.

At its core, the Playbook emphasizes:

- **Principles of Leadership** – Courage, clarity, collaboration, and accountability.

- **Practical Tools** – Step-by-step methods for building

skills, partnerships, and systems that dismantle barriers.

- **Blueprint for Action** – A structured sequence leaders can follow to move from vision-casting to implementation to measurable results.

Globally, I have seen how leaders succeed when they have both **a compass and a map**: the compass of vision to stay true to their values, and the map of actionable steps to navigate complexity. The Leadership Playbook & Blueprint provides both.

It is here, at this intersection, that *From Poverty to Prosperity* begins its deeper journey—using the Playbook as a foundation and the Blueprint as a roadmap for leaders ready to rise above charity and relief work, and step into their true role as architects of transformation.

DTD's Leadership Playbook & Blueprint

A Guide for Leaders and Aspiring Leaders to Break the Cycle of Poverty

I. The Four Pillars of Leadership

Every leader engaged in poverty reduction must be grounded in principles that guide decision-making, inspire others, and sustain momentum.

1. **Courage** – Leading when the stakes are high and resistance is strong.
2. **Clarity** – Defining vision with specificity and ensuring every action aligns.
3. **Collaboration** – Building coalitions across sectors, cultures, and geographies.
4. **Accountability** – Measuring results and being transparent about impact.

II. The Three Phases of the Blueprint

Phase 2: Action – Building the Bridge Between

Vision and Reality

- **Design Strategies**: Select interventions from the 14 poverty-breaking pathways (e.g., workforce development, parental empowerment).
- **Mobilize Resources**: Align people, funding, and partnerships to support the plan.
- **Implement Boldly**: Launch initiatives with both urgency and adaptability.

Leadership Tool: The **Action Matrix** – a tool to align actions with responsible parties, timelines, and resource needs.

Phase 3: Impact – Phase 1: Vision – Seeing Beyond the Present

- **Define the Future**: Articulate a vivid picture of prosperity for your community or organization.

- **Identify Barriers**: Pinpoint systemic, cultural, or economic blocks that perpetuate poverty.

- **Set Bold Goals**: Establish specific, measurable outcomes (e.g., increase college enrollment by 25% in 5 years).

Leadership Tool: The **Vision Map** – a one-page document outlining what success looks like in 5, 10, and 20 years.

Measuring What Matters Most

- **Track Outcomes**: Focus on generational results, not just immediate relief.
- **Evaluate Sustainability**: Ensure programs can endure leadership changes or funding shifts.
- **Scale and Replicate**: Expand successful models to new communities, industries, or nations.

Leadership Tool: The **Impact Dashboard** – a scorecard that tracks indicators like income mobility, educational attainment, community trust, and wealth growth.

III. The Leadership Pathways in Action

The Blueprint integrates the **14 pathways** introduced in earlier works. Leaders can adapt them based on context, but the Playbook insists they be interconnected rather than isolated:

- Skillset Development fuels Workforce Readiness.
- Parental Empowerment strengthens Educational Attainment.
- Civic Engagement amplifies Advocacy and

Leadership.

- Wealth Development locks in generational gains.

Leadership Insight: Leaders must think like **architects**—seeing how each pathway fits into the structure of a prosperous society.

IV. Action Checkpoints for Leaders

To ensure progress, the Playbook includes checkpoints at every phase:

- **Vision Checkpoint**: Does your community understand and share the vision?
- **Action Checkpoint**: Are the right people and resources mobilized effectively?
- **Impact Checkpoint**: Can you demonstrate measurable, sustainable change?

V. The Playbook Promise

The Playbook and Blueprint exist to simplify complexity and empower leaders. Whether you are a CEO, policymaker, educator, or grassroots organizer, this model gives you a **practical roadmap** to break poverty in ways that last.

It is not about doing everything. It is about doing the **right things in the right sequence**—so that leadership turns vision into action, and action into lasting impact.

DTD's LEADERSHIP PLAYBOOK & BLUEPRINT

THE FOUR PILLARS OF LEADERSHIP

- Courage
- Clarity
- Collaboration
- Accountability

THE THREE PHASES OF BLUEPRENT

VISION → ACTION → IMPACT

VISION	ACTION	IMPACT
• Define the Future	• Design Strategies	• Track Outcomes
• Identify Barriers	• Mobilize Resources	• Evaluate Sustain-Bility
• Set Bold Goals	• Implement Boldly	• Scale and Replicate

THE LEADERSHIP PATHWAYS IN ACTION

Innate Skiliset Development	Youth Development Programs	Advocacy & Leadership	Leadership Training & Development
College Exploration & Development	Career Readiness Development	Business Education & Development	Workforce Development Education
Health & Wellness	Parental Program Development	Building & Sustaining Community Relationships	Sports, Education and Leadership

ACTION CHECKPOINTS FOR LEADERS

- Vision Checkpoint: Does your community understand and share the vision?
- Action Checkpoint: Are the right people and resources mobilized effectively?
- Impact Checkpoint: Can you demonstrate measurable, sustainable change?

www.ingramcontent.com/pod-product-compliance
Lightning Source LLC
Chambersburg PA
CBHW061000280326
41935CB00009B/778